Get Carter

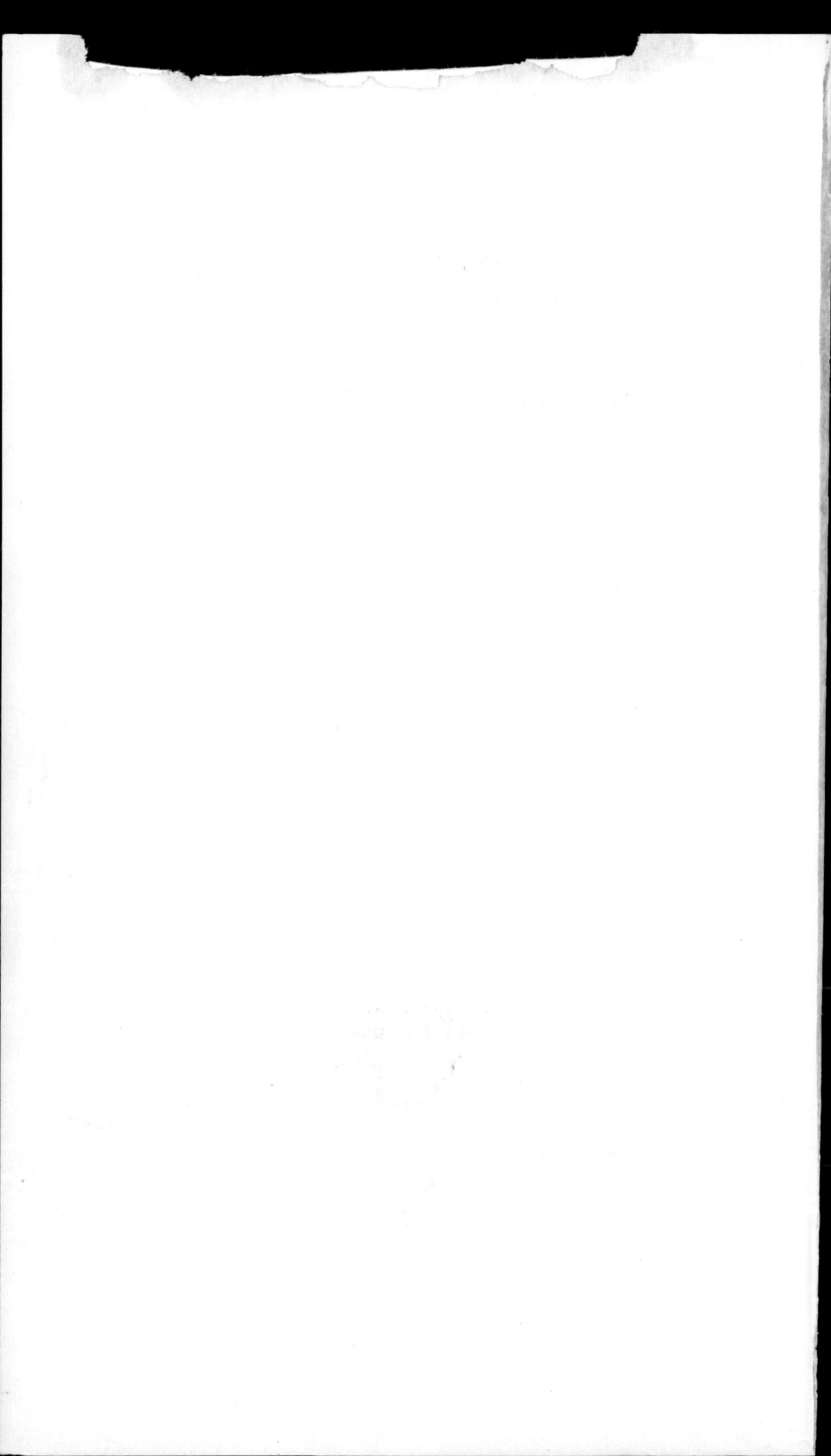

Get Carter

a screenplay by Mike Hodges

based on the novel Jack's Return Home
by Ted Lewis

SCRE 000I

SCREENPRESS BOOKS

First published in 2001
by ScreenPress Books
28 Castle Street, Eye, Suffolk IP23 7AW

Photoset by Parker Typesetting Service, Leicester

A CIP record for this book
is available from the British Library

ISBN 1 901680 32 0

For information on forthcoming ScreenPress Books,
contact the publishers at:
ScreenPress Books
28 Castle Street
Eye, Suffolk IP23 7AW

fax: 01379 870267
www.screenpress.co.uk

To Michael Klinger

Contents

Preface

The rain rained.

It hadn't stopped since King's Cross.

So began Ted Lewis's novel *Jack's Return Home*. That was its title when it was sent to me in 1969 with an offer to script and direct it as my first cinema flick. It was to star Michael Caine. *Carter's the Name* topped the title-page on my first draft. The novel was duly published in 1970 with its original title; then republished in 1971 as *Carter*. Strange, because by then the film was out and was called *Get Carter*. Elmore Leonard wouldn't have let that pass.

> *I was the only one in the compartment. My slip-ons were off. My feet were up.* Penthouse *was dead. I'd killed the* Standard *twice. I had three nails left. Doncaster was forty minutes off.*

That's the third paragraph of the novel; but already my script was deviating. Caine's Carter doesn't bite his nails. He takes white pills, mysterious nose drops, and fastidiously wipes his implements in the restaurant car of the train. This Carter is obsessional. This Carter reads a classy pulp paperback by Raymond Chandler, not because I wanted to compare him to Chandler's hero, as some dumb critics suggested, but as a portent. I knew Carter wouldn't live to see the end credits; indeed they would roll up over his dead body. I also knew that the hit-man who was to blow him away was sitting in the corner of the same compartment, already on his tail like a homing missile. The paperback is *Farewell, My Lovely*.

In my previous film, *Rumour*, made for television in 1969, the hero was a gossip columnist, one of the showbiz rat pack, and is first seen driving a flashy pink Oldsmobile along the Westway in London. In those days a cinema stood behind the flyover, its marquee peeping above the parapet. *Goodbye Columbus* was playing there. By carefully excluding *Columbus* from the shot, my hero is introduced with the word *Goodbye* writ large behind him. He, too, will meet his end via the trigger-finger of a hit-man. Portent or mordant humour? Both.

> *'Pint of bitter,' I said.*
> *He let his arms unfold, reached out for a pint mug and made his weary way to the pumps, and without putting anything more into it than it needed he began to pull a pint.*
> *'In a thin glass please,' I said.*

⊁ Caine's Carter points and doesn't say 'please'. If he had, I might have been spared twenty-five years of macho men, on learning I made the film, snapping their fingers at me with the same sinister authority. No wonder it was serialized in *Loaded* magazine last year; as a comic strip.

These examples of the many small changes between novel and script (all, I hasten to add, approved by Ted Lewis) lead inevitably to the big one. The locating of the story itself; the place where Carter's roots rotted as a child and adolescent; the blast furnace where his hardness and anger were cast.

> *Doncaster Station. Gloomy wide windy areas of rails and platforms overhung with concrete and faint neon. Rain noiselessly emphasizing the emptiness. The roller front of W. H. Smith's pulled hard down.*
> *I walked along the enclosed overhead corridor that led to the platform where my connection was waiting.*

The connection leaves for we know not where. A steel town with no name. I can't remember why I didn't locate the film in a steel town. Maybe because I didn't know any. I'd spent my early life in the chocolate-box environs of Salisbury and Bath; cities with soft centres. My blinkers were ripped away when I belatedly did my National Service at twenty-two. By some freak I ended up in the Royal Navy as an ordinary seaman. Few conscripts ended up in the navy; only I and one other joined HMS *Coquette*, an ocean-going minesweeper, living alongside men doing seven, fourteen, even twenty-one years' service. The lower deck became my university. *Coquette*, and later HMS *Wave*, were both leaders of the Fishery Protection Fleet. They took me to the Arctic and to

Iceland at the fag-end of the fish wars; but more importantly into every fishing port in the British Isles. Ashore, safe inside my matelot's uniform, I melted into a world of brutal Hogarthian intensity, and was mesmerized. These were the places I kept thinking of as I read *Jack's Return Home.*

Lowestoft. Grimsby. Hull. Each had been decimated by developers. The pubs, cafés and dodgy boarding houses gone. Thirteen years had passed. The producer, Michael Klinger, had insisted that he, his driver and Yank car take me on my recce up the east coast. My embarrassment, riding into these places in a Cadillac, matched only my despair at what I was seeing through its tinted windows. On the brink of returning south, I remembered sailing into North Shields. My memories of it were vivid. We pressed on and came to Newcastle. The visual drama of the place took my breath away. Seeing the great bridges crossing the Tyne, the waterfront, the terraced house stepped up each side of the deep valley, I knew that Jack was home. And although the developers were breathing down the Scotswood Road, they hadn't yet gobbled it up. We'd got there in time. But only just.

Now the film was about to part company with the novel. I began to weave into the script the amazing backdrop I had come upon. The pub opposite the station, reputed to have the longest bar in Europe, where Carter forgot to say *please.* Incidentally, the really observant will spot that the old man supping his brown ale has one finger more than the prescribed four! In the novel, the big shoot-up between Carter, Con McCarty and Peter the Dutchman, the boys sent from London to bring him back, took place outside Albert's house. In the film it's set around the ferry boat between North and South Shields. The Tyne Bridge is used for Carter's meeting with Margaret, his dead brother's girlfriend. The Swing Bridge is where he buys heroin to kill her and implicate Cyril Kinnear.

Cyril Kinnear was very, very fat. He was the kind of man that fat men like to stand next to. He had no hair and a handlebar moustache that his face made look a foot long on each side. In one way it was a very pleasant face, the face of a wealthy farmer or of an ex-Indian Army officer in the used-car business but the trouble was he had eyes like a ferret's.

Kinnear is played by John Osborne, famous author of famous plays and scripts such as *Look Back in Anger*, *Tom Jones* and *The Charge of the Light Brigade*. Osborne was tall, thin and hirsute. Re-reading the novel I now remember it wasn't just the locations I changed.

Instead of Carter bumping into Eric Paice in a pub, I set the scene at the racetrack. A wonderful betting shop I found in South Shields is where he finally catches up with Albert and knifes him to death. Here, a blind man laying a bet represents those characters in the film who literally turn a blind eye to what is going on around them. Just like the last eighteen years; only for real.

The high-rise car park and restaurant, epicentre of Cliff Brumby's shaky empire, the ugly unfinished concrete shell from which Carter tips him, I found in Gateshead. When Brumby's architects hear the approaching police sirens, one turns to the other and says, 'I'm not sure we're going to get our fees for this one.' At the time, I didn't realize how close I was sailing to the truth. Years later I was told the building had already been condemned as unsafe and was now demolished. True or not, it certainly felt right. Indeed, the more I explored the dark corners of the North-East, the more I began to sense the sickly smell of corruption. It was a smell I recognized; in the mid-sixties I'd been a producer/director on *World in Action*, Granada's investigative TV programme.

Instinct now drove me to look closer at a murder committed in Newcastle three years earlier. The body of Angus Sibbet had been found in a Jaguar parked under a bridge close to *La Dolce Vita* nightclub. He'd been shot. Two men, Dennis Stafford and Michael Luvaglio, were arrested and convicted. It was the motive for this killing that provided much background detail in the film, as well as an important location – Cyril Kinnear's home.

Luvaglio was the youngest brother of Vincent Landa, described by the *People* newspaper as 'the handsome and flamboyant boss of Social Club Services Ltd, one of the principal suppliers of fruit machines in the North-East'. It went on to accuse him of having 'milked' the fruit machines in 1,500 working men's clubs to the tune of £3,000,000. That's a lot of sixpences! As usual the tabloid never submitted its sums for scrutiny. Whatever the jackpot, it was sufficient for Landa to do a bunk with his wife and six children to his 'sunkissed villa' in Palma, Majorca.

Both Luvaglio and Angus Sibbet had been involved in extracting those sixpences. Sibbet got greedy; end of story; end of Sibbet. Poring over the cuttings I came across this one: 'Fruit-machine king to sell stately home.' It went on: 'The ten-roomed Dryderdale Hall, Co. Durham, into which 35-year-old Mr Landa moved four years ago from a corporation-owned semi at Peterlee, will be sold as soon as the estate agents settle details. The hall stands in 130 acres of woodland.' The report made Landa sound like Charles Foster Kane. With Xanadu on my mind, I contacted the agents and found that the property was still on the market.

Gloom and bad vibes were where the comparison ended. Evidence of the Landa's hurried departure lay about the miserable interior. The production designer kept bringing me things like children's drawing books and rolls of 35mm negative which he found strewn about the place. I still have them. The drawing books reveal a child obsessed by religion. Every page is scrawled with 'little prayers'. For example: 'Thank you Jesus for dieing on the cross for me. I will do what I am told and be as good as I can' and 'Lent. Jesus fass for 40 days in the desert for me. I too will do something for him every day.' I wonder how this devout child coped with a father on the run and an uncle convicted of murder, and if the fate of the two brothers is somehow reflected on the page daubed with: 'CAIN AND ABEL CAIN AND ABEL CAIN AND ABEL RIGHT NOW.' Looking at that page still makes my blood freeze.

It is ironic that Dryderdale Hall, previously the residence of Vincent Landa, should become the fictional home of the film's arch villain, Cyril Kinnear. We had to do very little to make it convincing. When Carter runs the gauntlet of Kinnear's bodyguards and bursts into the house, he hides in a back room, pressing himself against the wall. Look closely and you'll see the wall is papered with a kid's pattern of 'cowboys and Indians'. This reference to the myths of the 'Western' wasn't artful direction. It was already there. As I write, I wonder if Landa ever ran the video of Get Carter at his 'sunkissed villa' in Majorca. Or did the police finally manage to extradite him? I have no idea what happened to him.

> *I hear him jump down on the other side and begin to walk away. Then there is silence for a long time until I hear the car door slam again and the engine start up and I listen to the sound until it dies away and then there is nothing, nothing at all.*

So ends *Jack's Return Home*. Samuel Beckett wrote, 'In the beginning is the end – but we still go on.' And so it is with Caine's Carter. He's shot dead before our eyes; but still goes on. He is, of course, eternal; he's on film.

Mike Hodges

2001

Get Carter

EXT. PENTHOUSE APARTMENT. LONDON. NIGHT
Framed in the large picture window stands Jack Carter, alone, looking out at the night. He turns away as the heavy satin curtains close, wiping him from view.

INT. FLETCHER'S APARTMENT. NIGHT
A blinding beam of light cuts across the room. One pornographic slide after another hits the screen at the opposite end of the room. They show a dowdy group in some anonymous bedroom, frozen in various stages of a sexual orgy.
Gerald Fletcher is slumped on a sofa. His young wife, Anna, is curled up beside him.
Sid Fletcher, operating the projector's remote-control, has the same flaccid appearance as his twin brother.
Jack Carter, drink in hand, watches from an armchair.
Clunk. Another slide hits the screen. Gerald is getting turned on. He runs his hand along his wife's stockinged leg. Anna shudders momentarily. She obviously finds his touch repulsive. Carter watches Gerald's hand.
GERALD: (*removing the cigar from his mouth*) Bollock naked with his socks still on?
SID: (*thoughtfully*) They do that up North.
GERALD: What for? Protective purposes?
    He laughs.
SID: Ask me?
GERALD: Ask Jack. It's his old stamping ground.
    Carter turns sharply away to the cocktail cabinet. Lights and sweet music happen when he opens it.
    Clunk. The slide changes.
SID: Must be a bloody contortionist
    Still looking at the screen, Gerald continues.
GERALD: We don't want you to go up the North, Jack.

Jack and Anna look at each other momentarily. There is definitely something between them.

JACK: No.

Clunk. The slide changes.

GERALD: (*groans*) Not suede boots!

SID: Knock it off, Gerald.

GERALD: What? And get the clap?

Clunk. The slide changes.

You work for us, Jack. We have connections in those parts. I'd hate you to screw 'em up.

Clunk. The slide changes.

What's that? A python.

Sid laughs raucously.

Clunk. The slide changes.

What are you going for?

JACK: To find out what happened.

Clunk. The slide changes.

GERALD: Some hard nuts operate up there, Jack. They won't take kindly to someone from London poking his bugle in.

JACK: Too bad.

GERALD: I smell trouble, boy.

Clunk. The slide changes.

SID: The law was satisfied.

JACK: Since when was that good enough?

Clunk. The slide changes.

GERALD: Think again, Jack.

JACK: I will.

EXT. RAIL TRACK. DAY
Express train plunges into a tunnel. Blackness.
Begin titles.

INT.TRAIN COMPARTMENT. DAY
The compartment is full. Jack Carter sits in one corner, reading a Raymond Chandler paperback, Farewell My Lovely.

EXT. RAIL TRACK. DAY
The train speeds northwards. In the distance the stacks of a lonely power station belch a continuous stream of brown smoke.

INT. TRAIN CORRIDOR. DAY
Carter steadies himself as he comes along the corridor.

EXT. RAIL TRACK. DAY
A massive iron bridge crossing a river whips past. Its mesh sides create an almost hypnotic effect.

INT. TRAIN TOILET. DAY
Carter tips his head back and dispenses drops into his nose.

EXT. RAIL TRACK. EVENING
The train breaks from another tunnel. Evening light cuts across the track as the train hurtles on.

INT. TRAIN RESTAURANT CAR. EVENING
Carter pours himself a glass of water and takes out a small phial of brown pills. He swallows one.

EXT. RAIL TRACK. NIGHT
A chemical factory, brightly lit, passes by and the outskirts of the city appear.

INT. TRAIN COMPARTMENT. NIGHT
The train moves slowly along the platform and stops. Carter collects his coat and briefcase from the rack.

EXT. NEWCASTLE STATION. NIGHT
The street is fairly deserted.
Carter exits with other passengers from the train. He pauses and looks about before crossing to the pub opposite.

INT. THE LONG BAR. NIGHT
A couple of youths are playing records on the juke box. An old man sits in the corner reading a newspaper.
Carter enters through the swing door and a weedy barman comes to serve him.

CARTER: Pint of bitter.

> *The barman picks up a glass mug and begins to draw the*
> *beer. Carter snaps his fingers at him.*

In a thin glass.

> *The barman sighs petulantly, transfers the beer into a thin*
> *glass and puts it on the counter.*
> *A telephone rings. The second barman answers it.*

BARMAN. Is there a Mr Carter in the room?

CARTER. Yes.

> *Carter walks to the far end of the bar and picks up the*
> *receiver.*

Hello? (*pause*) Margaret? (*pause*) Why the hell aren't you
here? (*He lights a cigarette.*) What time? (*pause*) Is Doreen at
the house? (*pause*) Who's with him then? (*pause*) When can I
see you? Will you be there tomorrow? (*pause*) Now listen,
Margaret . . .

> *The line goes dead. Carter hangs up.*

INT. FRANK CARTER'S HOUSE. HALL. NIGHT

A key hanging inside the letter box starts to move upwards and
out through the flap. A moment later, the door opens. Carter is
standing at the bottom of a flight of stairs in a worker's terraced
house. He closes the door and climbs the stairs.

FRANK CARTER'S HOUSE. LANDING. NIGHT

Carter moves cautiously. His eyes scan the peeling wallpaper, the
mildew on the banisters. A roof leak hits an unseen bucket with
depressing regularity.

INT. FRANK CARTER'S HOUSE. BEDROOM. NIGHT

An unmade bed with pyjamas on it, a beaten-up wardrobe, a
dressing table and chair are about it. Carter hears a vehicle
stopping on the street below. He eases back the ancient net
curtain. Two men in a Land Rover are looking up. They see him
and quickly drive off.
Carter looks around the room. On top of the wardrobe there's an
old shotgun. He reaches up and brings it down. Memories flood

CARTER: PINT OF BITTER.
[THE BARMAN PICKS UP A GLASS MUG.
CARTER SNAPS HIS FINGERS.]
~~IN~~ A THIN GLASS!

back. He reaches up again and finds a box of cartridges. More memories. Jack and Frank grew up here. He leaves the gun on the bed and returns to the landing.

INT. FRANK CARTER'S HOUSE. LIVING ROOM. NIGHT
Pitch black. An overhead light snaps on to the face of a dead man: Frank Carter. He is lying in a coffin. His eyes are closed, his skin made-up, like porcelain.
Carter stands over the coffin. He gently touches his brother's crossed hands and folds the shroud over his face. He exits, turning out the light and closing the door. Darkness returns.

INT. 'LAS VEGAS' BOARDING HOUSE. ENTRANCE HALL. NIGHT
The landlady, Edna Garfoot, is climbing the stairs. She's well built, sexy, experienced. Carter follows with his baggage. He watches her appreciatively from behind.
CARTER: I won't be using the room tonight.
EDNA: (*stops and turns*) I see.
CARTER: I'm staying with a friend.
EDNA (*continuing up the stairs*) Her husband docks tomorrow, does he?
CARTER: (*smiles*) It's not like that, luv.
EDNA: It never is.

INT. BOARDING HOUSE . BEDROOM. NIGHT
The door opens and the light goes on. It's a big room overlooking the road, furnished cheaply but comfortably.
Edna and Carter enter, talking.
EDNA: Are you a traveller?
CARTER: (*smiling*) Definitely.
EDNA: (*surveying the room*) Will this do?
CARTER: (*looking around*) Very nice. (*He takes his wallet out.*) I'll pay you for tonight as well.
EDNA: Don't be bloody silly. You're the first since Monday.
CARTER: You sure?
    Carter gives her the money.
EDNA: Ta.
CARTER: (*feeling the mattress*) I'll bet this one's seen some action.

Carter smiles and looks straight at her. Edna returns his look,
dead pan.
EDNA: I'll give you the key when you come down.
She closes the door.

INT. FRANK CARTER'S HOUSE. LIVING ROOM. DAY
Carter moves around the coffin as he shaves. His electric razor is
plugged into the lamp above his dead brother.

INT. FRANK CARTER'S HOUSE. LIVING ROOM. DAY
The coffin lid is being screwed down.
Carter stirs a cup of instant coffee while watching the undertakers
at work.
CARTER: Was he in bad shape?
UNDERTAKER: They come worse.

INT. HEARSE. DAY
The hearse is parked outside the row of terraced houses. A
youthful undertaker is minding it. He turns and looks through the
back window as a young girl walks up the street.
Doreen Carter is sixteen and, like most girls of her age, tries to
look older. She wears all the right gear but it's cheap and doesn't
fit properly. Her long hair is lank. There's something sad and
embarrassing about her appearance. The young undertaker
watches as she enters Frank's house.

INT. FRANK CARTER'S HOUSE. LIVING ROOM. DAY
The door opens slowly. Doreen stands there looking at the coffin.
Carter sees her.
CARTER: Doreen?
    She seems mesmerized by what's going on.
    All right, are you?
    Doreen doesn't answer.
    Been staying with a friend?
    Doreen nods. The undertaker coughs and thrusts another
    screw into the coffin.
CARTER: Sorry about your father.
DOREEN: (*pause*) Yeah.

9

CARTER: Tell me, Doreen, did the police say anything?
DOREEN: (*dazed*) They said he was drunk.

INT. HEARSE. DAY
*The young undertaker is still in the hearse listening to the radio.
In the driving mirror he sees the Land Rover moving slowly up
the road. It stops by the house. Two men suss the scene and drive
off.*

INT. FRANK CARTER'S HOUSE. LIVING ROOM. DAY
CARTER: How's school?
DOREEN: I left last year.
CARTER: Oh, what you doing now?
DOREEN: Working at Woolworths.
CARTER: That must be interesting.
DOREEN: Yes.
    Carter and Doreen look at each other awkwardly.
CARTER: What you going to do? Live with Margaret?
    *Doreen looks at him nervously, shakes her head and fumbles
    in her bag for a cigarette.*
    Carter continues, slightly indignant.
    Well, why won't you come with us to South America? My
    fiancée won't mind. (*pause*) Your dad would have wanted it.
    The undertaker puts the final screw in.
UNDERTAKER: (*to colleague*) Get Hughbert up, will you? (*to
    Carter*) We're ready now, sir.

EXT. FRANK CARTER'S HOUSE. DAY
*The undertakers struggle with the coffin down the narrow
staircase into the street. Outside Carter and Doreen wait with two
men. Eddie Appleyard, a middle-aged man, is wearing a shabby
tweed suit, cap and black tie. Keith Lacey is a young barman who
worked with Frank.*
EDDIE: We weren't sure where it was taking place, like.
CARTER: Nice of you to come.
EDDIE: No. Frank was a good bloke.
KEITH: He was that.
EDDIE: One of the best.

INT. LIMOUSINE. DAY
Through the windscreen of the following limousine Carter can see his brother's coffin in the hearse as it moves slowly through the streets of the city. Sitting in front on fold-out seats are Eddie and Keith.

KEITH: I couldn't believe it when I heard.
> *Carter is suddenly attentive.*

CARTER: What?

KEITH: I mean, I was surprised when he didn't turn up for work. He was always on time.

CARTER: Did you work with him, Keith?

KEITH: At the Half Moon.

EDDIE: (*not to be left out*) It's a bloody funny thing. You know a bloke for six bloody years and all the time he's as calm as gentle Jesus. (*pause*) Then he goes and does a thing like that. (*He shakes his head.*)
It's a bloody funny thing.

CARTER: (*quietly*) Yeah. A bloody funny thing!

EXT. CREMATORIUM GATES. DAY
As the cortège drives into the crematorium, it passes the Land Rover parked outside. The same two men who passed Frank's house are in it. A long and expensive-looking funeral cortège passes out as they move up the driveway.

INT. CREMATORIUM. DAY
Carter, Doreen, Eddie and Keith are in the front pews facing the catafalque on which Frank's coffin rests. The vicar is already midway through the solemn words of the 'committal' when a woman enters. The clunk of her high heels cuts through the silence. Everybody looks round.

CARTER: (*whispering to Doreen*) Is that Margaret?
> *Doreen nods. Frank's coffin sinks out of sight.*

INT. CREMATORIUM COMMITTAL CHAMBER. DAY
Two men in long grey coats wait in silence. The coffin appears. Expertly, they take it and swing it on to a trolley. They push it up

*the wide corridor towards the furnace. One of the men starts
whistling cheerfully.*

EXT. CREMATORIÚM. DAY
*Margaret is thirtyish, blonde, attractive in a tarty kind of way.
Her heels are too high and she is wearing a cheap pair of
sunglasses. She walks quickly away, down the cloisters, past the
memorial tablets and urns.*
Carter comes out of the chapel and sees her.
CARTER: Margaret.
    Margaret stops and looks round. Carter joins her.
    I thought you weren't coming.
MARGARET: Changed me mind.
    *They face each other in silence. Margaret looks past Carter
    and sees Doreen watching them at the end of the cloisters. She
    turns away and starts walking slowly. Carter moves with her.
    Margaret continues nervously.*
    Everyhing go off all right?
CARTER: Fine. (*pause*) I want to talk to you.
MARGARET: What about?
CARTER: Doreen.
    *Margaret stops in her tracks and looks back at Doreen. She's
    still watching them.*
MARGARET: (*adamantly*) She's nothing to do with me.
CARTER: (*puzzled*) What do you mean? You've been Frank's bird
    ever since her mother cleared off. You're closer to her than
    anyone.
MARGARET: (*shaking her head*) No. No. It's not like that. I've
    got a husband, you know.
    Margaret starts walking again, fast.
    Carter catches hold of her arm and stops her.
CARTER: Hold it! Hold it! (*Looking her in the eye*) Who killed
    Frank, Margaret?
MARGARET: (*nervously*) Killed? I don't know anything about it.
    She moves off rapidly. Carter catches up with her.
CARTER: Really.
MARGARET: I must go. I'm in a hurry.
CARTER: I want to talk to you later.

MARGARET: I can't.

CARTER: Tomorrow morning, then?

    Margaret dithers.

MARGARET: Well, all right then. Twelve o'clock on the Iron Bridge.

    Margaret walks off as calmly as she can, her high heels clicking as she goes. Carter watches her disappear. Doreen watches too.

INT. CREMATORIUM COMMITTAL CHAMBER. DAY

Frank's coffin is slid inside the furnace. Flames start to lick it as the steel trap closes.

INT. THE HALF MOON PUB. DAY

It's a large room with a horseshoe bar in the centre, a real boozer. A handful of hard drinkers are already in position.

Carter, Doreen, Keith and Eddie are sitting alone. Their table is already covered with glasses. Doreen appears to be slightly drunk on Babycham, Eddie on whisky and Keith on beer. Carter is stone-cold sober.

EDDIE: Absent friends. (*He raises his glass and drinks, then continues thoughtfully.*) You don't think he might have done it on purpose?

KEITH: What? You mean, like, kill himself?

    Eddie and Keith look at each other.

    Doreen watches them. She is getting very upset by the conversation.

    Naw. Frank? Kill himself? You what?

    Carter stares at Keith, who is getting uncomfortable.

    I mean, what for?

CARTER: That's what I was wondering.

KEITH: Come off it. Frank was . . . well . . . straight. He had no worries I know. Hell, we worked together every day for a year. It would have showed.

CARTER: Why would it?

KEITH: It just would. He was always the same.

CARTER: Since when did he drink whisky?

KEITH: Don't know.

CARTER: Nobody seems to know.

Doreen is now crying openly.

EDDIE: (*finishing off his drink*) Bloody good bloke. One of the best.

DOREEN: (*blurts out*) How would you know? (*She suddenly jumps up and empties her glass in Eddie's face.*) Or you? Or you? None of you knew. *I* knew. He was me dad.

She runs off out of the door crying. Keith goes to follow. Carter puts his hand out to restrain him.

CARTER: Let her go. She'll be OK. (*to Eddie*) Sorry about that.

EDDIE: (*wiping his face with a handkerchief*) Don't worry. She's bound to be upset.

CARTER: (*to Eddie*) Have another?

EDDIE: No. I'll be off now. I should be at work.

Eddie stands up, cap in hand. Carter pulls out a wad of money.

CARTER: Look, look. (*He peels off a note.*) Get your suit cleaned.

EDDIE: No. It's all right.

CARTER: (*standing, pushes the note in his top pocket*) Thanks for coming.

EDDIE: Frank was a good bloke. It's the least I could have done.

Eddie leaves.

CARTER: You work here, Keith?

KEITH: Yes.

Carter thinks for a moment, then leans forward to Keith.

CARTER: Keith, if anybody comes in here and asks for me, you let me know. Right?

KEITH: Right.

CARTER: I'm at the Las Vegas. Behind the dance hall. (*He casts an eye around the bar.*) Do you know a man called Albert Swift?

KEITH: Yeah. He comes in here a bit.

CARTER: Where would I find him?

KEITH: Today? At the races. He always goes.

Carter takes out his phial of pills.

How'd you know Albert?

CARTER: Went to school with him. (*smiles*) He was leader of our gang. He'll know what's going on in this town.

EXT. RACE TRACK. DAY
*The rain has just stopped. Bookies and punters lower their
umbrellas. Horses thunder towards the finishing post. Turf flies in
all directions as the jockeys whip their mounts in a last desperate
effort and the crowd roars.*

EXT. TRACK ENCLOSURE. DAY
*Albert Swift is standing by a bookmaker's marking his race card
with a biro. A hot dog is sticking out of his mouth, like a cigar.
A man of about thirty-five, he appears much older, probably from
an excess of booze and women. He looks up, and his mouth drops
open, the hot dog falling to the ground. He has seen Carter.*

EXT. TRACK ENCLOSURE. DAY
*Carter is pushing his way along the line of bookies, all the time
looking about him. The track loudspeaker announces the winner
of the last race.*

EXT. TRACK ENCLOSURE. DAY
*Albert pales. He holds his race card in front of his face and
disappears into the crowd. As he moves off, his foot steps on the
hot dog and tomato ketchup oozes out.*

EXT. TRACK SADDLING ENCLOSURE. DAY
*Carter stands alone, casting an eye over the punters. His eyes rest
on someone the other side of the saddling ring: Eric Paice.
Dressed in a grey chauffeur's uniform, cap, dark glasses and
gloves, he is standing close to three well-heeled-looking men with
binoculars and shooting sticks.
Horses for the next race are being led around the enclosure.
Carter approaches from behind. He looks at Eric closely before
speaking.*
CARTER: Grey suits you, Eric.
    Eric swings round, startled.
ERIC: Good God!
    Carter smiles.
CARTER: Is he?
ERIC: Jack Carter.

CARTER: (*amused*) Eric. Eric Paice.

ERIC: What you doing around here then?

CARTER Didn't you know this is my home town?

ERIC: No, I didn't know that.

CARTER: Funny, that.

Carter takes out his cigarettes. Eric takes one.

ERIC: Thanks. So what're you doing? On your holidays?

CARTER: No. I'm visiting relatives.

ERIC: Oh, that's nice.

CARTER: It would be. If they were still living.

ERIC: Meaning what?

CARTER: A bereavement. A death in the family.

ERIC: Oh, I'm sorry to hear that.

CARTER: That's all right, Eric.

Carter flicks his lighter and gives Eric a light.

ERIC: Well, well. Small world, isn't it?

CARTER: Very. (*pause*) So, who you working for these days Eric?

ERIC: Oh, I'm straight. (*Indicating uniform*) Respectable.

CARTER: (*smiling*) What are you doing? Advertising Martini?

ERIC: Oh, you've been watching television.

CARTER: Yeah. (*pause*) Come off it, Eric. Who is it?

Eric smiles back.

Brumby?

Eric shakes his head.

Kinnear?

Eric shakes his head.

ERIC: What's it to you anyway?

CARTER: I've always had your welfare at heart, Eric. Besides which, I'm nosy.

ERIC: That's not always a healthy way to be . . .

CARTER: And *you* should know, if I remember rightly.

A track announcement interrupts them.

So you're doing all right then, Eric. You're making good.

ERIC: Making a living.

CARTER: Good prospects for advancement, is there? A pension? (*He can't resist it any longer. He lifts the sunglasses off Eric's nose and looks into his eyes.*) Do you know, I'd almost forgotten what your eyes looked like.

Eric stares back.
They're still the same. Piss holes in the snow.

ERIC: Still got a sense of humour?

CARTER: Yes, I retained that, Eric. (*He moves towards the saddling ring and turns to Eric.*) Do you know a man called Albert Swift, Eric?

ERIC: Can't say I do.

Carter looks across at the track.

CARTER: Don't miss the start on my account.

EXT. RACE TRACK. DAY
Starting gates slam open and the horses leap out.

INT. HIRE CAR. AFTERNOON
Carter is driving along a country road. Ahead, two cars are between him and a Cadillac with dark-tinted windows. The Cadillac turns on to a minor road. Carter follows.

INT. CADILLAC. LATE AFTERNOON
Eric Paice is driving. In the back sit the three men seen with him at the race track. The drinks compartment is open and they are helping themselves to champagne. Racing results come over the car radio.

INT. HIRE CAR. LATE AFTERNOON
Carter follows the Cadillac at a safe distance. It turns into a driveway. Carter slows down and reads a sign by the entrance: The Heights. He drives on and parks.

EXT. THE HEIGHTS. LATE AFTERNOON
Carter comes through a wooded area. He pauses by a lake, now overgrown with weeds. A big man stands tossing stones into the water. Carter silently picks up a dead branch then runs at the man. Carter whacks him on the head and he collapses unconscious into the lake. Carter moves on towards the house. Marty and Ray the two men previously seen in the Land Rover, are playing with an Alsatian on the spacious lawn fronting the house. It's a Victorian building surrounded by acres of woodland.

19

Carter breaks from the trees and darts for the side door. One of the men notices and shouts after him.

INT. THE HEIGHTS. LATE AFTERNOON
Carter runs into the house and slips into a small service room. Ray and then Marty charge inside but miss seeing Carter.

INT. THE HEIGHTS. SITTING ROOM. LATE AFTERNOON
A game of poker is in progress. Seated around the table are the three men with Eric at the race track. With them is an elegant man, Cyril Kinnear. On the sofa are Glenda, a sexy-looking young woman, and Eric Paice.
Ray bursts in.

RAY: Carter's here.
Eric jumps up.
ERIC: Where?
RAY: I don't know.
ERIC: You stupid shit!
Carter walks past Ray, blowing him a kiss.
Kinnear watches with some amusement.
KINNEAR: You see what it's like these days, Jack.
You can't get the material.
Carter looks at Eric.
CARTER: Yes, I can see your problem, Mr Kinnear.
KINNEAR: Sit down, Jack. (*pause*) I could weep. I really could.
Sometimes I think I'll retire. Just piss off to the Bahamas and
let somebody else employ them. (*to girl*) Glenda, get Jack a
drink. What is it, Jack?
CARTER: (*to Glenda*) Scotch, please.
KINNEAR: (*to bouncer*) Piss off, Ray.
Ray closes the door behind him.
Glenda brings Carter his Scotch. He looks at her as she sits beside him.
Eric told me of your bereavement.
CARTER: Yep.
KINNEAR: Do you know, I never knew he worked in one of my
places!
CARTER: No? Funny that. Neither did I.

KINNEAR: If I'd known, I'd have fixed him up with something better.

CARTER: Yeah.

KINNEAR: Nasty way to go.

CARTER: Yes.

One of the three men sitting around the table with Kinnear gets impatient. Peter, Les and Harry are well-heeled, middle-aged, northern businessmen.

HARRY: Are we here to play cards or talk about the old days?

KINNEAR: Harry! Jack, I don't want to be rude, but these men have brought a lot of money with them. Glenda, you don't offer a man like Jack a drink in those piddling little glasses. Give him the bloody bottle. (*He picks up his cards.*) Now, where are we?

Harry keeps a cold, wary eye on him.

Oh . . . I think I'll stay as I am.

HARRY: (*shaken*) You're bluffing, you bastard!

KINNEAR: That's what you pay to find out. Right, Jack?

CARTER: Right. If you can afford it.

HARRY: (*to Carter*) Thought you were going soon.

CARTER: Soon. When you've lost your money. Won't take long.

HARRY: Clever sod, aren't you?

CARTER: Only comparatively.

KINNEAR: Harry, I don't like to push, but could you let us know how much your hand's worth?

Harry looks at his cards. Glenda tucks her legs up, making sure that Carter gets an eyeful.

GLENDA: You know Sid Fletcher?

CARTER: What?

GLENDA: You know Sid Fletcher?

CARTER: I work for him.

GLENDA: Do you?

CARTER: (*amused*) Yes, I do.

Carter looks back at the table. Kinnear pushes in some money.

HARRY: What's that? A hundred?

KINNEAR: That's right, Harry.

HARRY: Your hundred, and another hundred.

'Bandit' fiddle: Clubs act

WORKING MEN'S CLUBS which were "milked" of more than £3 million in The Great Fruit Machine Fiddle are all set for a dramatic new move to cut their losses.

They expect to get the go-ahead this week. Then they will stop all hire-purchase payments being made under illegal agreements.

The "pay-up freeze" has been decided on by Durham Branch of the Club and Institute Union, which has 350 members, many of them victims of the great fiddle.

Action day will be next Friday, following a meeting of the branch's executive — and the "stop paying" instruction will be sent out to 100 clubs.

These clubs still have tens of thousands of pounds outstanding under hire-purchase agreements.

But after taking legal advice on contracts, the union has decided that further payments are unjustified because many of the clubs have been grossly overcharged.

At the same time Mr. Gordon Bagier, Labour M.P. for South Sunderland and chairman of the unofficial Parliamentary committee on gaming and gambling, is seeking an interview with Home Secretary Mr. Roy Jenkins.

Mr. Bagier has the 250-page dossier on the fruit machine fiddle compiled by "The People" and he intends to hand this over to the Home Secretary and discuss it with him.

Meanwhile there have been repercussions in the one-armed bandit empire of 35-year-old Mr. Vincent Landa.

Last week bailiffs moved into the Sunderland offices of his Social Club Services Ltd. and took possession of fruit machines and office furniture.

Later they were auctioned to raise cash to meet a series of debts incurred by the company and others controlled by Mr. Landa. The sale produced £750—of which more than £500 will go to Sunderland Corporation for rates.

The rest will help to meet some outstanding debts, for a series of writs totalling thousands of pounds—one has been issued by Gateshead British Legion Club—have been served on some of Mr. Landa's firms.

Other activity includes business changes. The Coinmatics firm of Newcastle-upon-Tyne—for which Mr. Landa's father Mr. Frank Luvaglio works—has assumed responsibility for the maintenance and other contracts for machines issued by Social Club Services.

And Mr. Frank Hoy, managing director of Cam Automatics Ltd., Seaham, based rivals of the Landa one-armed bandit business, has sold his interests to a Newcastle group.

Fruit-machine king to sell stately home

THE country mansion of fruit-machine king Vincent Landa is to be put up for sale.

The ten-room Dryderdale Hall, near Wolsingham, Co. Durham, into which 35-year-old Mr. Landa moved four years ago from a corporation-owned semi at Peterlee, will be sold as soon as the owner's representatives and estate agents settle details.

The hall stands in 130 acres of woodland.

Antiques have stood in packing cases for almost a year while he has been living in 10-roomed luxury apartment in Palma, Majorca.

At a sale in Sunderland last month, fruit machines from Social Club Services Ltd., one of Mr. Landa's businesses, raised almost £3,800. This went to paying off Sunderland corporation rates and clearing the firm's debts.

[handwritten annotations:]

STILL ON THE MARKET. MAR '71.

RESEARCH LOCAL CRIME CONNECTED TO MURDER! MAR. '71

FIND CUTTING THAT LEADS TO LOCATION

REAL VILLIAN'S HOME BECOMES FICTIONAL ONE — 'THE HEIGHTS'

KINNEAR: NASTY WAY
TO GO.
CARTER: YES.

Kinnear lays more cash on the table.
What's that?

KINNEAR: That, Harry? That's another hundred – twenty-five pounds notes of the realm.

HARRY: Three hundred altogether?

KINNEAR: Three hundred altogether, Harry.
Glenda attracts Carter's attention again.

GLENDA: I know him too.

CARTER: Who?

GLENDA: Sid Fletcher.

CARTER: (*sending her up*) Oh, do you?

GLENDA: (*dumb*) Yes.

CARTER: No, do you really?
Carter turns to the table yet again.
Harry nervously puts another hundred on the table. Kinnear purses his lips.

KINNEAR: I'll follow that and go two hundred.
Harry looks sick.
You can always see me, Harry.
Harry sweats and then smiles nervously.

HARRY: All right. Two hundred.

KINNEAR: (*raises an eyebrow*) Ha.
Kinnear takes a wad of notes out of his pocket. Glenda shifts herself on the sofa.

GLENDA: Yes. I met him last year.

CARTER: Go on.

GLENDA: Oh yes. When he came up on business.

CARTER: Really?

GLENDA: He came to see Mr Kinnear.

CARTER: No.
Carter, getting bored, looks back at the game.

HARRY: (*panicking*) What's that?

KINNEAR: That's six hundred pounds, Harry. Two hundred to follow you, and I've raised it four hundred.
Harry sweats some more.

HARRY: Four hundred?

KINNEAR: That's right.

HARRY: You're not seeing me?

KINNEAR: No.
Harry smiles nervously. He counts some money out.
HARRY: I'll see you, then.
KINNEAR: Calling my bluff, are you, Harry?
Harry nods.
Glenda speaks, but this time Carter keeps his eyes on the table. Kinnear lays out his hand – a hearts flush, queen high.
GLENDA: We went about together.
CARTER: Really?
GLENDA: Yes, while he was here.
CARTER: While he was here. You went about together?
GLENDA: He was here for four days.
CARTER: Was he?
GLENDA: Could you do me a favour?
CARTER: Yeah, I'll do you a favour.
GLENDA: Could you please put my glass on the table?
Carter smiles and does just that.
KINNEAR: Oh, come on, Harry. I haven't won, have I? Go on, you're pulling my leg.
Kinnear leans across to pick up Harry's cards. Harry grabs them and puts them in the pack. Kinnear turns to Carter.
How about that, Jack? Old Harry thought I was having him on.
HARRY: Shut up.
Carter gets up from the sofa.
KINNEAR: Not going, Jack?
CARTER: I have to. Things to see to.
KINNEAR: Of course, of course. Well, any time, just drop by.
CARTER: Yeah, I'll do that. (*He points at Harry.*) Told you it wouldn't take long, didn't I?
Eric opens the door and follows him out.

INT. THE HEIGHTS. HALLWAY. EVENING
Carter moves towards the front door.
ERIC: Jack! I didn't like that.
CARTER: You should have told me who you were working for.
ERIC: Cyril didn't like it, either.

CARTER: Oh, Cyril, eh? So it's all girls together, is it?
ERIC: He's thinking Sid and Gerald won't like it much when they
hear you've been sticking your nose in.
Carter carries on walking to the front door. He opens it.
CARTER: He's right. Tell him to save the cost of the phone call.
Carter leaves. Eric signals Ray to follow him.

EXT. SCRAPYARD. DAY
*Huge metal claw catches hold of an old car and lifts it like it was a
toy. The yard is beside the River Tyne. In the distance a train
crosses the Iron Bridge.*
*Carter is examining a beaten-up Hillman when the yard owner,
Billy Laws, approaches.*
BILLY: (*suspicious*) What do you want?
CARTER: What happened to this car?
BILLY: What's it got to do with you?
CARTER: This is my brother's car.
BILLY: Oh ay?
CARTER: Yeah.
BILLY: Well, he drove it into the river.
CARTER: Was the steering faulty?
Billy shakes his head.
What about the brakes?
BILLY: Fine. Nowt wrong with them.
CARTER: How'd it happen, then?
BILLY: He was drunk. Drunk as a lord.
CARTER: Was he?

INT. THE HALF MOON. NIGHT
*A big, busty pub singer is performing on the small stage. A trio on
her right plays a good, grinding, up-tempo number.*
*Carter comes through the door. He pushes his way through the
packed drunken crowd to the bar. Keith serves him.*
KEITH: What you having, Jack?
CARTER: Large Scotch.
*Carter watches the singer. The customers cheer and whistle.
Keith returns with the Scotch. He looks nervously around and
speaks to Carter quietly.*

26

KEITH: Heard of a man called Thorpe?

CARTER: Old Thorpey? Haven't seen him in a long time.

KEITH: (*picking up Carter's money*) That's what he was saying about you.

> *Keith takes the money to the till. The music grinds away. Keith returns.*

Said he'd heard you were up in town. Wondered if I knew where you was staying. Wanted to look you up. Old time's sake.

CARTER: That's nice. What'd you tell him?

KEITH: Nowt.

CARTER: Good lad.

> *Carter watches the singer, then finishes his drink.*

See you later.

KEITH: Where you off to?

CARTER: (*smiling*) Las Vegas.

> *Carter makes for the door. The singer is now moving through the tables. She pauses to give some man a kiss. Everybody cheers.*
>
> *The woman sitting with the man snaps. She picks up his glass of beer and throws it over the singer; then grabs her hair and pulls her to the ground.*
>
> *Carter stops to watch. The two women roll on the floor, punching and scratching.*
>
> *Carter smiles and leaves.*

EXT. ALLEY IN TOWN CENTRE. NIGHT

On the corner is a neon-lit snack bar. Doreen and another young girl are sitting inside sucking milk shakes. Somewhere a drunk is singing. His voice echoes up the alley.

Carter draws alongside and notices Doreen. He stops and watches her. She hasn't seen him so he goes to the window and knocks on it. She looks up and he beckons her outside. Reluctantly, she comes.

CARTER: (*gently*) You all right now?

DOREEN: Yeah.

CARTER: You coming to South America?

27

DOREEN: No.
Carter's hurt and slightly irritated by this rejection.
CARTER: Where you going to live, then?
DOREEN: At me friend's house.
CARTER: Where's that?
DOREEN: Wilton Estate.
CARTER: Nice family, are they? Church-goers and all that?
Doreen nods.
Good. I'm off tomorrow, so I don't suppose I'll see you
again. (*He pulls out a wad of money, and peels off some
notes.*) There. Go and get your hair done.
DOREEN: (*can't believe it*) Thanks.
He lifts her chin with his finger and looks at her.
CARTER: Be good. And don't trust boys.
*Doreen blushes and turns away. She rushes back to the snack
bar with the money to show her friend.*

INT. BOARDING HOUSE. HALL/SITTING ROOM. NIGHT
The front door opens and Carter enters.
*Standing on the hall table is a small wooden casket with an
envelope taped to it. Carter pockets the envelope and picks up the
casket.*
EDNA: (*off-screen*) That was left for you this evening.
Carter walks past her into the sitting room.
What is it?
CARTER: My brother, Frank.
EDNA: Is he staying the night?
CARTER: Funny. (*He puts the casket on a side table.*) Can I phone
London?
EDNA: It'll cost you.

INT. FLETCHER'S HOUSE. BEDROOM. NIGHT
*Anna is undressing. She's alone. Pulling the short black-silk
underslip over her head, she stands in front of a long mirror, clad
only in black panties, bra and tights. She looks at herself
appreciatively. The phone rings. She flops on the bed and picks up
the receiver.*
ANNA: Hello.

A voice speaks on the end of the line.
How I miss you. (*She stretches herself out sexily and smiles.*)
Stop it, darling.

INT. BOARDING HOUSE. SITTING ROOM. NIGHT
It's a cosy room. Carter is on the telephone. Edna sits in a rocking chair.
CARTER: (*looking at Edna*) I fancy you. I wish I was touching
you right now . . .
Edna turns towards him. Carter fixes her with his eyes. Edna rocks herself gently. Carter continues softly.
. . . making love to you. I want to stroke you and kiss you
all over. Where are you?

INT. FLETCHER'S HOUSE. BEDROOM. NIGHT
Anna is lying full-length on the bed.
ANNA: In the bedroom.
Carter speaks on the other end.
My black underwear.

INT. BOARDING HOUSE. SITTING ROOM. NIGHT
Edna rocks backwards and forwards.
CARTER: (*quietly*) The sexy, silk ones?
Anna replies. He continues softly.
Take your bra off. (*pause*) No, go on.

INT. FLETCHER'S HOUSE. BEDROOM. NIGHT
Anna unhooks her bra. There's a flash of breasts.

INT. BOARDING HOUSE. SITTING ROOM. NIGHT
The scene as before.
CARTER: Now hold them. Gently.

INT. FLETCHER'S HOUSE. BEDROOM. NIGHT
Anna's hands cover her breasts. Her head moves slowly from side to side, eyes closed.

INT. BOARDING HOUSE. SITTING ROOM. NIGHT
Scene as before.
CARTER: Slowly. Imagine it's me.

INT. FLETCHER'S HOUSE. BEDROOM. NIGHT
Anna's hand caresses the inside of her leg. Her head rolls from side to side slowly. She's breathing heavily.
Cross-cut between Edna's head rocking backwards and forwards and Anna's head moving from side to side.
CARTER: (*voice-over*) When we're in South America, we'll make
    love in the sun. Roll over . . . and make love again . . . and
    again . . . For me . . . I fancy you . . .
    The speed of the cutting builds.

INT. FLETCHER'S HOUSE. BEDROOM. NIGHT
Suddenly the door opens and Gerald comes in. He sees Anna groaning on the bed.
GERALD: What's the matter? You got gut trouble or something?
    Anna sits up abruptly and puts her hand over the receiver.
ANNA: No, darling. Just doing some exercises. (*into telephone*)
    Listen, Janet, Gerald's just got in, so I must ring off. (*pause*)
    Yes. Yes. I'll come tomorrow.

INT. BOARDING HOUSE. SITTING ROOM. NIGHT
Scene as before.
CARTER: Save it till Sunday. I'll be back then.
    Carter replaces the receiver. He still holds Edna's eyes. She
    rocks to and fro. The rocker creaks.
    The front door bell breaks the mood.
    That'll be for me.

INT. BOARDING HOUSE. HALL. NIGHT
Carter opens the door. Keith is outside. He's sweating. His tie is somewhere round the back of his neck and his suit is covered with dirt.
KEITH: Thorpey. They were waiting for us in the car park.
CARTER: How many?

KEITH: Four of them.

> *Carter pulls Keith inside and turns out the light. A Ford Zodiac comes along the road. It stops. Four faces peer into the darkness where they're standing. Nobody gets out. The back window winds down. Thorpe's nervous voice floats out.*

THORPE: Jack?

CARTER: Good evening.

THORPE: I'd like a word with you, Jack.

CARTER: That's nice.

THORPE: Confidential, like.

CARTER: You stay in the car. I'll come and listen. (*He leaves the darkness and walks to the car.*) What you want to tell me, Thorpey?

> *Thorpe holds out his hand.*

THORPE: I've been asked to give you this.

> *He hands Carter a railway ticket. Carter smiles.*

Train goes at four minutes past twelve. You've just got time.

CARTER: That's very kind of somebody. Who do I have to thank? (*pause*) What happens if I miss the train?

THORPE: I've been asked to make sure you don't.

CARTER: Oh, really. You're getting very optimistic in your old age, aren't you, Thorpey?

> *One of the men inside mutters.*

MAN: Let's stop pissing about.

THORPE: Are you coming, Jack? It'd be best.

> *Carter tears the ticket in half and drops it in the gutter.*

Right lads.

> *The front passenger door starts to open. Carter grabs it and pulls it wide open. With all his force, he slams it against the man as he gets out. The window shatters over his head. Blood spurts everywhere.*
> *The driver panics. He accelerates away as the man in the back is getting out. His foot is trapped in a safety belt. He's upended and dragged along the tarmac, his head dangerously close to the back wheel. His yells make the driver brake.*
> *In the confusion Thorpe escapes from the car and makes off. Carter spots him and begins to run.*

CARTER: (*roars*) Thorpe!

*Thorpe turns into the main road. He makes for the dance hall
and disappears inside. Carter follows.*

INT. DANCE HALL. NIGHT
*The dance floor is full, mainly with miniskirted girls, their
handbags at their feet. A rock band play mechanical music to
match the dancing.*
*Thorpe vanishes into the crowd circling the floor. Carter arrives.
He scans the place, then sees Thorpe as he disappears down into
the gents' lavatory.*

INT. DANCE HALL. GENTS' LAVATORY. NIGHT
*Carter enters. There's no sign of Thorpe. He checks the cubicles
until he finds the one that's occupied, then goes into the next one.
He climbs on the seat and looks over the partition. Thorpe is
sitting down looking at the door. Carter quietly leans across and
pulls the chain. Thorpe jumps up, terrified.*
CARTER: Time's up, Thorpey.
        Carter smiles.

EXT. BOARDING HOUSE. NIGHT
*Keith kicks broken glass into the gutter while he waits. Edna's
next-door neighbour, an old woman, watches. Carter and Thorpe
come down the street.*
CARTER: Hello, Keith. (*pause*) Stay there, Thorpey.
        He knocks on Edna's door. It flies open. Edna is furious.
EDNA: What the bloody hell do you think you're at?
CARTER: (*smiles*) I'm sorry.
EDNA: You don't look it.
CARTER: No. Really, I am.
EDNA: Don't come that bloody flannel with me. If you're a
        traveller, I'm bloody Twiggy. (*She points at Thorpe.*) And
        who's he?
OLD WOMAN: What's going on? Have you no thought for others?
CARTER: We're going inside.
EDNA: Inside? Why should I give house-room to your sort?
CARTER: Up the stairs, Keith. The door on the right.
OLD WOMAN: Everybody knows you, Edna Garfoot. Everybody

33

knew there'd be trouble when you moved in.
Carter, Keith and Thorpe enter the house.
EDNA: You keep your trap shut, Ma.
OLD WOMAN: I'll send my old man to see you!
EDNA: And wouldn't he love it!

INT. BOARDING HOUSE. HALL. NIGHT
Carter, Thorpe and Keith are climbing the stairs. Carter stops to pick up Frank's casket. Edna rushes in and slams the door.
EDNA: Where do you think you're going?
Carter opens the door to his room.
CARTER: Why don't you go and make us all a nice cup of tea?
Carter shoves Thorpe into the room. Keith follows.
EDNA: And what you going to do?
CARTER: Make us a nice cup of tea and I'll tell you. I might even let you watch.
EDNA: I'll call the police.
CARTER: (*he knows she fancies him*) No, you won't.
Carter closes the door.

INT. BOARDING HOUSE. BEDROOM. NIGHT
Carter carefully places the casket on the chest of drawers.
CARTER: Well now, Thorpey. It seems I've got a secret benefactor. (*He moves into the room and opens his briefcase, which is lying on the bed.*) It's nice to know that. Isn't it, Keith? (*He takes out a bottle of whisky.*) There's only one trouble, I don't know who to thank.
Thorpe looks longingly at the bottle of Scotch. Suddenly Carter punches him hard in the stomach. He grunts and collapses into a chair.
Now, I want to know who it is, Thorpey.
Carter tosses the whisky bottle to Keith and continues wearily.
All right. If you like, Thorpey, we'll stop mucking about. Somebody doesn't want me poking my nose into something and I happen to know what that something is. (*pause*) Now stand up.
Thorpe looks at him, terrified. Slowly he stands. Carter grabs

him by the testicles and applies preasure. Thorpe screams.
Who paid you to see me off?

THORPE: I can't Jack. How can I?

CARTER: Yes you can.

Carter applies more pressure. Thorpe screams.

THORPE: No, don't Jack, don't.

CARTER: Who sent you, Thorpey?

THORPE: (*desperate*) Brumby!

Carter gives him a final squeeze and lets go. Thorpe groans and slips to the floor, doubled up in agony.

CARTER: There you are, you see. Now you could, couldn't you? (*pause*) and quickly.

There's a knock on the door. Carter lets in Edna, who is carrying the teatray.

Ah, Edna, come in. Join the tea set.

KEITH: Who's Brumby?

CARTER: Cliff Brumby. Ever been to Westsea?

Keith nods.

Ever been into an arcade there and put a penny in the slot machine?

KEITH: Yeah.

CARTER: Ten to one, it belonged to Cliff Brumby, and like as not the bloody arcade as well. Right along the coast. Isn't that right, Thorpey?

Thorpe drags himself painfully to a chair.

Where's he living these days?

THORPE: He's got a new place at Burnham.

CARTER: Address?

THORPE: On the Durham Road. The Pantiles.

EDNA: (*furious*) Suppose you tell me what the bloody hell's going on. It's *my* house, you know.

CARTER: Yes, Edna, and I must say you've been great about the . . .

EDNA: Stick the soft soap. Let's be having it.

Thorpe's plaintive voice interrupts.

THORPE: Can I go now?

CARTER: You must be joking. (*to Keith*) Keep him away from the telephone. I'm going out for a bit.

EDNA: Now just a minute . . .
CARTER: Ta-ra.
THORPE: Don't let on I told you, for God's sake.
Carter laughs and closes the door.

EXT. THE PANTILES. NIGHT
It's a large, new, ranch-style house, set back from the road. The front garden is a landscape gardener's nightmare, with its phoney brick and wrought-iron wishing well, porcelain dwarfs, lily pond, the lot. Fairy lights hang over everything.
There's a party going on. Lights are on in every room and the rock music is loud. The drive is lined with sports cars.
Carter parks and gets out.
Out of a side door a young man stumbles towards the lily pond. There, he promptly throws up. Carter watches from behind a tree. His attention shifts to the white Bentley turning into the drive. It brakes sharply and the driver jumps out.
Cliff Brumby has been to a police ball. He is impeccably dressed in tuxedo and white scarf. Now he's hopping mad.
BRUMBY: Jesus wept!
Mrs Brumby cowers in the passenger seat.
MRS BRUMBY: Now, Cliff, don't get mad.
BRUMBY: I'll murder the little bitch!
MRS BRUMBY: Cliff . . .
Brumby roars up to the front door, banging it furiously. A young woman in a party dress, expecting to greet a latecomer, is stunned to see who it is.
SANDRA: Daddy!
BRUMBY: That's right, bloody Daddy.
SANDRA: I wasn't expecting you until three o'clock.
BRUMBY: And this is what you call having a few friends back for coffee, is it?
Brumby pushes past her into the house.
Running bloody riot over my bloody furniture, drinking my bloody booze . . .
The rest is lost as he disappears inside. He then powers out through the side door
. . . spewing over my fucking goldfish.

CARTER WATCHES
FROM BEHIND A TREE.
HIS ATTENTION SHIFTS
TO THE WHITE BENTLEY
TURNING INTO THE
DRIVE.

*He aims a kick at the young man's backside, sending him
face-down into the lily pond.*
*Mrs Brumby gets out of the car and hovers for a moment. As
she approaches the house, people pour out. Brumby appears at
the door with a boy pulling up his trousers.*
MRS BRUMBY: Cliff . . .
Brumby throws the boy out.
BRUMBY: Shut up, Phyllis. (*He walks back into the house.*) Sandra!
*Mrs Brumby goes into the house and closes the door. Brumby
passes an upstairs window as Sandra locks herself in a
bedroom.*
Sandra! Unlock the door, you bitch.
*Carter pauses outside the front door and listens to the row
going on upstairs. He opens the door and goes in.*

INT. THE PANTILES. NIGHT
*Carter passes silently through the hall into the large sitting room.
Mrs Brumby is sitting in an armchair.*
Brumby is still yelling at his daughter upstairs.
CARTER: Good evening.
Mrs Brumby jumps.
The front door is open.
MRS BRUMBY: (*standing*) Who are you?
CARTER: I'm an old friend of Cliff's. I want to see him.
Mrs Brumby looks at her watch irritably.
It's urgent.
MRS BRUMBY: What's it about?
CARTER: Business
MRS BRUMBY: I know all about Cliff's business.
Carter moves further into the room.
CARTER: Yeah, well, tell him the Fletchers sent me.
*Mrs Brumby is uncertain what to do. Carter sits in an
armchair to make his point. She leaves. A moment later
Brumby storms into the room.*
BRUMBY: What the bloody hell's all this?
Carter doesn't move.
You know what the bloody time is! (*pause*) It's two o'clock
in the bloody morning!

38

CARTER: I know.

BRUMBY: Well?

Carter still doesn't move.

The wife says the Fletchers sent you.

Carter just looks at him. Weighing him up.

What's so bloody important it couldn't wait till the morning?

Carter starts to laugh. He realizes Thorpe has lied to him.

Brumby isn't his man.

Listen, I'm not in the mood for bloody silly buggers.

Carter stands.

CARTER: I made a mistake.

BRUMBY: What?

CARTER: I made a mistake.

BRUMBY: What about?

CARTER: Never mind.

Brumby looks confused.

BRUMBY: It's *not* business?

Carter moves to the door.

CARTER: See you.

Brumby moves between him and the door.

BRUMBY: Listen, I don't like it when some hard nut comes pushing
his way in and out my house in the middle of the night.

Carter again makes to leave. Brumby stops him.

Bloody well tell me who sent you.

CARTER: You're a big man, but you're in bad shape. With me, it's
a full-time job. Now behave yourself.

*Brumby swings at him. Carter moves away from the punch,
then applies several sharp blows to Brumby's head and neck.
Brumby groans and collapses into the armchair, hurt.
Carter walks into the hall and out of the front door.*

CARTER: Good night, Mrs Brumby.

EXT. 'LAS VEGAS' BOARDING HOUSE. NIGHT
*Carter walks up the deserted street to Edna's place. He finds the
front door unlocked.*

INT. BOARDING HOUSE. HALL. NIGHT
Carter enters cautiously. There is no sound. He closes the door

quietly and pauses at the foot of the stairs. Still there is no sound.
He waits. A sudden rustle attracts his attention. Quietly, he moves
to the sitting-room door.

INT. BOARDING HOUSE. SITTING ROOM. NIGHT
Carter switches on the light. Edna is pressed against the far wall,
holding a poker. Her dress is torn and her hair dishevelled. When
she sees Carter, she sighs with relief.
EDNA: You sod.
CARTER: They came back?
EDNA: (*sarcastically*) No.
    Carter helps himself to a glass of water from the tap. Edna
    looks at her torn dress.
    Look at this. You bastard.
    Carter puts the glass on the table.
    You don't care a stuff, do you?
    Carter takes out his phial of pills.
CARTER: I'll buy you another.
    Carter swallows a pill.
EDNA: What about the lad? They took him away.
    Carter shrugs his shoulders.
    What'll they do to him?
CARTER: Don't ask me.
    Edna rubs her wrists.
EDNA: They bloody hurt me.
CARTER: You're lucky. They *kill* as well.
EDNA: (*mocking him*) And what about you? Did you kill
    Brumby?
    Carter shakes his head.
    Thorpey nearly died laughing.
CARTER: That little shit!
EDNA: What about Keith?
CARTER: What about Keith?
EDNA: What you going to do?
CARTER: Pension him off.
EDNA: You're a bastard.
CARTER: (*angry*) What am I supposed to do? I don't know where
    they've taken him. Do you?

Edna shakes her head.
So shut up.
EDNA: What's that gun doing in your room? Suppose I phoned
   the police and told them there's a bloke staying in my hotel
   who's planning to shoot somebody?
CARTER: You wouldn't.
EDNA: How'd you know I wouldn't?
CARTER: (*smiling*) 'Cos I know you wear purple underwear.
EDNA: What's that supposed to mean?
CARTER: Think about it.
   *Carter takes hold of her torn blouse and rips it open. She is
   wearing purple underwear.*

EXT. BOARDING HOUSE. DAY
*It's Sunday morning. A girls' marching band rehearses on the
wasteground in front of the terraced houses. The Pelaw Hussars
march back and forth carrying their proud banner, led by the
drum majorette.*

INT. BOARDING HOUSE. DAY
*Above the bed hangs a sign: 'What would Jesus say?' In the bed
lie Carter and Edna. The distant sound of the marching band
helps them surface.*
EDNA: Are you awake?
CARTER: No.
EDNA: Do you want breakfast?
CARTER: You must be joking. I never eat breakfast. (*pause*) Did
   you sleep well?
EDNA: Uh-huh.

EXT. BOARDING HOUSE. DAY
*The Pelaw Hussars keep on marching. The back of their banner a
stiring motto:* For Youth and Valour.

INT. BOARDING HOUSE. DAY
Scene as before.
EDNA: Did you sleep well?

CARTER: Yes, thank you.
He puts his arm around her and moves on top.

EXT. BOARDING HOUSE. DAY
As the band executes another movement, a red Jaguar slides to a halt outside Edna's house. Two men get out. Peter the Dutchman and Con McCarty are definitely not local lads. They look, and are, lethal. They try Edna's front door. It opens.

INT. BOARDING HOUSE. DAY
Scene as before.
CARTER: Are you tired?
EDNA: No. Are you tired?
CARTER: No. I'm not tired. (*pause*) Do you eat breakfast?
Edna laughs. They start to make love. Gently.
Below the undulating bedsprings rests a large chamber pot and, beside it, Carter's shotgun. Beyond is the bedroom door. It opens slowly and the two men enter. Only their legs are visible.
CON: (*off-screen*) Put us in it, Jack.
Carter is off the bed, and Edna, in a flash. Edna screams and tries to stop the bedclothes following Carter on to the floor. Peter and Con stand beside the bed smiling. Peter is a queer and dressed fancy in a leather coat, wide-bottomed trousers and a loud silk scarf. His hair is bleached blond. Con is more traditional, more butch. He's in a camelhair overcoat, suit and tie. Both are in their thirties.
PETER: Don't let us interrupt you, Jack.
CARTER: I might have guessed.
CON: Sorry about this. But there you are. Orders are orders.
CARTER: And what orders would they be, Con?
Carter's hand runs over the carpet. It's going towards the chamber pot instead of the gun.
CON: Gerald phoned us in the middle of the night, said he'd heard you've been making a nuisance of yourself.
PETER: We've got to take you back to London.
CON: He said it'd be doing him a big favour.
Carter's hand finds the chamber pot and quickly moves on towards the gun.

43

We know why you're all steamed up, and so do Gerald and
Sid.
PETER: But they have to be diplomatic.
Carter pulls out the gun and jumps up.
CARTER: Right. Now take me back to London.
CON: (*smiling*) It'd be best if you got dressed first.
Carter moves around the bed towards them. He's naked.
Put it away, Jack. You know you won't use it.
PETER: The gun he means.
Both men are laughing.
CARTER: Out.
*Peter and Con back down the stairs. Peter looks up at
Carter's cock.*
PETER: If Anna could see you now.
CARTER: Out.
CON: Now, Jack. Be reasonable. You know we're going to take
you back – sooner or later.
CARTER: Out.

EXT. BOARDING HOUSE. DAY
Con is the first to emerge from the front door.
CON: Mind you don't catch cold.
Peter follows.
PETER: I hope she's got understanding neighbours.
Then Carter comes out, shotgun held across his chest.
CON: See you when you've got your drawers on.
*The old woman next door chooses that moment to come out
for her milk. As she straightens up, she sees Carter. The bottle
flies from her hand and smashes on her doorstep. Carter, never
taking his eyes off Peter and Con, slowly backs into the house.*

INT. BOARDING HOUSE. BEDROOM. DAY
*Carter watches from the window as he pulls on his jacket. The gun
lies across the armchair. Outside, he can see Peter and Con talking
by the Jaguar. Con exits.*
Edna, now in her dressing gown, enters.
CARTER: Do us a favour?
EDNA: What, and get myself beaten up again?

CARTER: No chance of that.

EDNA: Not much.

CARTER: They're friends of mine.

EDNA: And that'll make me feel better?

CARTER: I don't want to get rough, do I?

Carter picks up the gun. He hands Edna his case and the casket.

INT. REAR OF BOARDING HOUSE. DAY

Edna comes out of the back gate into an alley, carrying the casket and case. Con emerges from his hiding place holding a handgun.

CON: Hold it! Where do you think you're going?

Carter appears from the gate next door, covering Con with the shotgun.

CARTER: Strawberry Fair.

He takes Con's handgun and signals him to go into Edna's yard.

In. Turn right. (*He points the gun at the coalshed.*) Open that door.

Con unbolts the door.

And go inside.

Con goes in. Carter closes and bolts the door. He moves quickly back to Edna and the car.

EDNA: What you going to do?

CARTER: I'm going to sit in the car and whistle 'Rule, Britannia'.

Carter jumps into the car.

EDNA: You coming back?

CARTER: How could I stay away?

The car roars off.

EXT. BACK ALLEY. DAY

Washing hangs behind each house as far as the eye can see. Carter drives full tilt through it, collecting towels and sheets on the windscreen.

EXT. EDNA'S YARD. DAY

The coalhouse door is getting a terrible battering. It finally gives and Con bursts out. He runs into the alley, following after Carter.

EXT. BOARDING HOUSE FRONT. DAY

Carter's car screeches as it corners from the alley on to the road.
Peter is leaning against the open door of the Jaguar. When he sees
Carter coming straight at him, he scarpers for the pavement.
Carter hits the Jaguar's door at speed, tearing it off. It flies up and
crashes on to the tarmac as Carter careers over the wasteground.
Soon he is out of sight.
Con comes running. Peter is looking at the damage.

PETER: Where were you, then?

Con sees what's happened to the car and is not pleased.

CON: Bollocks.

EXT. BACK STREET. DAY

Carter pulls up outside a house and gets out. He takes the washing
off the car's bonnet, and throws it into a neglected garden.

EXT. FRONT DOOR. DAY

Carter presses the bell. The door's opened by a young man,
Shamir.

CARTER: Keith in?

SHAMIR: (*shouts*) Keith.

No answer. Shamir watches Carter as he walks into the hall.

CARTER: (*off-screen*) Which is his room?

INT. KEITH'S ROOM. DAY

Carter enters and closes the door. Keith is in a bad way, his face
like a piece of raw steak. He is lying on a bed, still in the clothes of
the night before.

CARTER: What happened to you, then?

KEITH: How'd you find me?

Keith lifts his head painfully from the pillow.

CARTER: Did they give you a rough time?

KEITH: No. (*He lowers his head to the pillow.*) You bastard. You
    knew they'd come back.

CARTER: No, I didn't. (*pause*) Does Albert Swift still live over the
    ferry?

KEITH: Get knotted.

CARTER: All right. All right. I want to square things with you first.

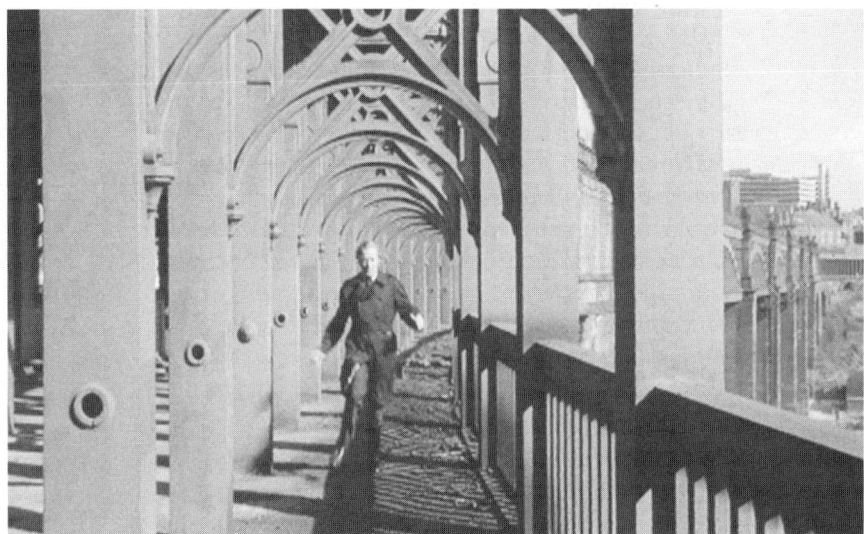

KEITH: Oh yes? How?

Carter takes out of his wad of money. Keith's bloodshot eyes watch him through the surrounding puff of flesh.

Stuff it! My girl friend's coming from Liverpool tonight. Nice surprise, isn't it?

CARTER: I'm sorry. Here. This'll pay for a course in karate.

He throws some money on the bed. Keith tries to kick it off, but it's too painful. He clutches his testicles.

KEITH: Frank said you were a shit and he was bloody well right.

Carter turns to leave.

Keith continues, crying and angry.

You even screwed his wife, didn't you?

Carter shuts the door, leaving Keith shouting after him.

The poor bastard didn't even know if the kid was his.

He falls back on to the bed, crying out in pain.

EXT. RIVERSIDE. DAY

A wide road runs alongside the Tyne. It passes below the vast steel bridges that link the two parts of the city. A car park lies at the foot of the 'Iron Bridge'. Carter pulls up and parks. He gets out and moves quickly.

EXT. THE IRON BRIDGE. DAY

The bridge is a massive structure. The traffic lanes are flanked each side by pedestrian walkways. It is here that Carter and Margaret have arranged to meet.

CARTER: How were things between you and Frank?

MARGARET: He was all right to me.

CARTER: Nothing more? Just another feller?

MARGARET: Nicer than most.

CARTER: But he was just another feller, wasn't he?

MARGARET: Yes.

CARTER: Though nicer than most?

MARGARET: Yes. I can't help the way I am.

CARTER: (*ignoring the statement*) Why'd you see him so regular?

MARGARET: Once a week?

CARTER: I call that regular.

MARGARET: He was gentlemanly. I like that.

CARTER: Once a week you like a gentleman?

MARGARET: (*angrily*) Look, I'm me, right. You're not. We are what we are, like it or not. (*She turns and walks slowly along the bridge.*) Why all the bloody needle?

CARTER: What was bugging Frank?

MARGARET: He wanted me to leave Dave and marry him. Last Friday I told him it wouldn't work. Dave would have killed us both! (*pause*) He followed me home and kicked up a stink in the street. (*pause*) I had to tell Frank I couldn't see him any more. It was getting too dodgy. That was on Sunday. (*She stops and looks over the bridge.*) He said he'd kill himself. I was frightened what you might do.
They look at each other for a moment. Carter shakes his head. He gently takes the sunglasses from Margaret's face and folds them up.

CARTER: I don't believe you, Margaret. Frank wasn't like that. (*pause*) I'm the villain in the family, remember?

MARGARET: It's the truth.
Carter snaps her glasses in two and throws them away.

MARGARET: It is. Honestly.

CARTER: (*shouting*) You bloody whore. Frank was too careful to die like that. Who killed him?

MARGARET: I don't know nothing.
Carter holds her arm. She winces like she's been hit before.

CARTER: Listen, the only reason I came back to this craphole was to find out who did it. And I won't leave until I do. You understand?
Behind Carter Peter's Jaguar comes slowly along the bridge. It stops. The passenger side is a gaping hole.

CON: Hello, Jack.
Carter swings round to see them, then swings angrily back to Margaret.

CARTER: You bitch! It was you who told them I was here, wasn't it?
He smacks her hard across the face. Margaret crys out. The car draws alongside. A steel mesh separates the pedestrian way from the traffic, so the two men can't get to Carter until he reaches the end of the bridge. Con leans out, his usual cheery self.

49

CON: Peter's very upset about his car. He's going to shit all over you.

CARTER: I'll catch up with you later, Margaret.

And with that he vaults over the handrail on to a corrugated roof. Con jumps out of the Jaguar.

PETER: (*shouts above the revs*) Come on, get in.

Con does and they race off.

EXT. WASTELAND. DAY

Carter arrives at the top of some narrow, steep, overgrown steps leading down to the river road, where his car is parked. He leaps down the steps as the Jaguar screeches to a halt at the top.

Con leaps out of the Jaguar and gives chase. Peter backs the Jaguar and roars off.

EXT. RIVER ROAD. DAY

Carter comes running down the steps with Con not far behind. He arrives at the river road. In the distance, he can see his parked car.

As he nears the car park, Peter's Jaguar comes down the hill. It's going to cut Carter off from his car.

A Sunbeam Alpine sports car waits there. Its engine roars into life and it races out of the car park. It reaches him just before the Jaguar and slows down.

GLENDA: Over here, Jack.

Carter sees that the driver is Glenda. The hood is down, so he vaults into the car as it accelerates off.

The Sunbeam swings round, narrowly missing the oncoming Jaguar, and roars away. Peter hasn't a chance. He's facing the wrong way and has little room to manoeuvre.

Glenda laughs as the car swings wildly around a corner at the top of the hill.

INT. SUNBEAM. DAY

Every movement Glenda makes is sexually charged: manual gear changes, steering, even braking. Carter can't take his eyes off her.

GLENDA: You didn't know you had a fairy godmother, did you?

CARTER: No. I didn't know that.

GLENDA: A fairy godmother, all of your own. Aren't you lucky?

CARTER: So where are we going, Princess?

GLENDA: To the demon king's castle, of course.

CARTER: Of course. Where else?

The car screams off the road into a multi-storey car park.

INT. MULTI-STOREY CAR PARK. DAY

Glenda really puts her foot down. The car hurtles around each deserted floor.

CARTER: How'd you know where I'd be?

GLENDA: You were seen parking your car. The demon king waves his wand and I was dispatched to bring you to him. Lucky for you I waited.

CARTER: Very lucky, I should think. You're drunk!

GLENDA: Nasty.

CARTER: He must have been pretty sure I'd come.

GLENDA: Oh, he was. He told me a magic spell that would make you come.

CARTER: (*smiling*) And what was that?

GLENDA: We're there now.

She brakes to a split-second stop.

INT. PENTHOUSE RESTAURANT. DAY

It's one large empty concrete box with big picture windows all the way round. Wires are hanging from the ceiling and walls where the lights will eventually be fixed.

A tall figure stands at the opposite end, facing the setting sun. He is just a silhouette.

Carter and Glenda enter and walk towards the man. The silhouette turns as he nears it. It's Brumby.

BRUMBY: A new venture of mine. It's going to be a restaurant. (*pause*) Do you like it?

CARTER: Yes.

BRUMBY: Last night, after you'd gone, I did a little bit of asking around. Seeing as you weren't very forthcoming. (*pause*) It seems that you are concerned about the death of your brother? (*pause*) I got to thinking it would be nice if the bloke you were after was the same bloke I wanted off my

back. (*pause*) You know my life. Machines. The arcades. Nice business. Looks after itself. People put money in. I take it out. Not much rough stuff. It's a business that makes me very happy. But recently, I've had a spot of bother. (*pause*) One of my lads gets a bit over-anxious and flogs some machines in a club that's already got some. The upshot is I've had to eat shit and stop flogging my machines to other clubs. (*pause*) So far as I'm concerned, that's it. Apparently not. These people I've offended get the idea that it would be good to take over my whole outfit. (*pause*) So I'm worried. I can't fight them – I haven't that kind of set-up. But I've got to fix them before they fix me. Trouble is, if I try and they find out, I'm dead.

Brumby picks up a black briefcase. He holds it up to Carter.
Five grand. It belongs to you. Along with a little name I'm going to give you.

CARTER: What name?

BRUMBY: Kinnear. Cyril Kinnear. (*pause*) Kinnear did it.

CARTER: Why?

BRUMBY: I don't know. All I know is that people were shitting bricks up at his place last Saturday. Your brother's name was mentioned. Next day, he was dead.

CARTER: Why?

BRUMBY: I don't know. That's all I was told.

Carter takes a last look at Glenda and walks slowly back towards the entrance.

CARTER: That's not good enough.

BRUMBY: Christ, what . . .

CARTER: (*shouting*) Do me a favour. You don't really expect me to fix Kinnear on your say-so? (*pause*) Just because they tried to get me on you last night, don't think you can pull the same trick. Stroll on.

BRUMBY: Jack, you're wrong.

CARTER: Good afternoon, Mr Brumby.

Carter exits.

BRUMBY: Jack . . .

EXT. MULTI-STOREY CAR PARK. DAY

Carter steps out of the elevator as Glenda's Sunbeam comes down the bottom ramp fast. The car brakes hard and stops. Carter opens the door and gets in. Not a word is said.

INT. GLENDA'S APARTMENT. DAY

The apartment is one of many in a modern block and Glenda has only recently moved in. There is a mattress on the floor. A large mirror leans against the wall behind it and a film projector stands close to the window, which has makeshift curtains.
Carter and Glenda are on the mattress. The bedding is all over the place. They have just finished fucking.

CARTER: (*looking around*) Who's setting you up in this place?

GLENDA: Brumby.

CARTER: Is he coming here?

GLENDA: Don't worry. He's meeting the architects at the restaurant.

Carter plays with her hair.

CARTER: Aren't you scared Kinnear will find out?

GLENDA: He won't. He thinks I'm simple.

Carter kisses her neck.

CARTER: What does he want that bloody great country place for?

GLENDA: (*knowingly*) Entertaining.

CARTER: What kind of entertaining?

GLENDA: Now you're asking.

Carter looks at the film projector by the bed and points.

CARTER: Does Brumby get a kick out of that crap?

GLENDA: (*giggling*) Especially when I play the lead.

Carter wraps his arms about her.

CARTER: Did Kinnear say anything? After I'd left the other night?

Glenda sits up sharply.

GLENDA: That's why you waited for me.

CARTER: (*kissing her on the neck*) Not entirely. No.

GLENDA: You sure about that?

CARTER: Sure I'm sure.

Glenda pushes him away and gets out of the bed.

GLENDAL You bastard.

Glenda leaves for the bathroom. Carter, curious, looks at the film projector. It's loaded. He switches it on. A beam of light hits the opposite wall. He settles down to watch the film. The leader flashes by, then a title being chalked on a school blackboard: 'The Teacher's Pet'. A zoom back reveals Glenda, bare-breasted, holding the chalk. This is followed by a long shot of a young girl, dressed in school uniform, waiting at a bus stop. A car approaches and stops. A woman driver offers the girl a lift. The woman is Margaret. The identity of the girl not revealed.

INT. GLENDA'S BATHROOM. DAY
Glenda is in the bath. Lots of foam. The hot water is still running. She's smoking. She leans forward, turning off the tap.

INT. GLENDA'S APARTMENT. DAY
Carter is sitting up on the mattress, amused by the soft porn unfolding on the white wall in front of him.
The schoolgirl accepts the lift and the car drives off. The door to an anonymous apartment opens and Margaret comes in with the girl. Her school hat still hides her identity. Glenda is there to greet them.
The girl is very awkward. Glenda tries to make her relax, sitting her down and showing her a magazine.
Glenda brings her into a bedroom. She takes her own top off and goes to do the same with the girl. She takes her hat off. A close-up shows that it is Doreen.
Carter tenses but never flinches from what's happening in the film. Margaret comes into the bedroom and feigns shock at what she sees. She slaps Glenda and they start fighting, eventually rolling off the bed.
The apartment door opens and a man smoking a big cigar comes in.
Carter sits up. It's Albert Swift.
Albert opens another door, looking for someone. He leaves. Another door opens and he's in the bedroom. He sees the two women fighting on the floor, but on the bed is his prize: Doreen. Carter watches.

55

Doreen bites her nails and looks terrified. Reflected in the mirror behind Carter is the image of Albert taking off his trousers. The reel runs out and flaps like a fish. Carter doesn't move. Tears form in his eyes. He looks old and defeated. His is a wasted life. Then the anger that drives him explodes again and he throws back the bedclothes.

INT. GLENDA'S BATHROOM. DAY
Carter, now dressed, moves slowly towards her in the bath.
CARTER: I want to give you an Oscar.
GLENDA: (*laughs*) You've been watching the film.
CARTER: Tell me about the girl.
GLENDA: What girl?
CARTER: The young girl. Who pulled her?
GLENDA: I don't know.
CARTER: Was it Albert?
GLENDA: Shouldn't think so.
CARTER: Is it one of Kinnear's films?
GLENDA: Yeah.
CARTER: Who set it up? Eric?
GLENDA: Yeah.
CARTER: Then he must have pulled her.
GLENDA: Expect so.
CARTER: Did my brother Frank find out?
GLENDA: Your brother? What you talking about?
      Carter's fury bursts. He's out of control. He seizes Glenda and plunges her under the bathwater, holding her there.
CARTER: You're a lying bitch.
      Carter lifts her up, out of the water. She is spluttering, nearly drowned.
      Now tell me the truth.
GLENDA: The girl's name was Doreen. That's all I know.
CARTER: And you didn't know her last name?
GLENDA: No.
CARTER: Well, it's Carter. That's my name. (*pause*) And her father was my brother. And he was murdered last Sunday. Now get up and get dressed.
      He pushes her ahead of him.

EXT. GLENDA'S APARTMENT BLOCK. DAY
Carter manhandles Glenda towards her Sunbeam. He opens the boot.
CARTER: Get in.
   Glenda climbs in and he slams the boot shut. The car scorches away.

EXT. JETTY. TYNE FERRY. DAY
Carter parks the sports car as the ferry docks. He moves down the gangway towards it.

INT. CAFÉ. DAY
A girl with a baby in a pram is having a cup of tea. The door slams open. There's Carter.
CARTER: Where's Albert?
   The girl is numb with fear, unable to answer. Carter grabs her by the throat.
   Where's Albert?
   The girl is frozen with terror. He lets go as suddenly as he grabbed her.
   I know where I'll find him.

EXT. BACK STREET. DAY
Carter walks fast. There's the sound of a phone being dialled. It's the girl in the café.
GIRL: (*voice-over*) Eric, he's come for Albert. (*pause*) I don't know. (*pause*) On the ferry, I reckon.
   Carter reaches the front of a betting shop. He walks in.

INT. BETTING SHOP. DAY
Carter closes the door. Race results and odds are coming over the Tannoy. He moves into the shop until he reaches Albert Swift. Albert is making out a betting slip and doesn't see him.
CARTER: Hello, Albert.
   Albert looks like he's going to be sick.
ALBERT: Hello, Jack. (*snivelling*) I don't know anything, Jack.
CARTER: Yes, you do, Albert. Talk or I'll kill you.
ALBERT: I know. I know.

Carter sees a door at the back. There's a sign for the toilets.
CARTER: Do you want to go to the toilet, Albert?
At first Albert doesn't understand.
Do you want to go to the toilet, Albert?
This time it clicks. Albert moves to the door and Carter follows.

EXT. BETTING SHOP BACKYARD. DAY
Carter turns to close the door. Albert runs for it. He reaches the high double-gate at the end. It's locked and he tries to climb it. No luck. Carter easily pulls him down. Albert faces him.
CARTER: You can't get away from me, Albert.
ALBERT: I know.
He feels for his cigarettes but can't find them.
For Christ's sake, give us a fag.
Carter takes out his cigarettes. Albert takes one.
I didn't know who Doreen was. Thought she was just another bird.
CARTER: Did Eric Paice pull her?
ALBERT: Yes.
CARTER: How?
ALBERT: I dunno. He's got his ways. He knows Margaret.
CARTER: When did *you* find out?
ALBERT: A couple of weeks back.
CARTER: How?
ALBERT: No choice. I had a visit from somebody.
CARTER: Who?
ALBERT: Cliff Brumby. He'd seen the film. He wanted to meet Doreen.
CARTER: And you told Brumby?
Albert nods.
Who killed Frank?
Albert doesn't answer.
Do you want to be dead, Albert?
ALBERT: Last Sunday afternoon, Eric and two of his boys arrive with Frank and tell me that he's rumbled. Somehow, he's seen the film and was about to shoot his mouth off. They ask me for some whisky and start forcing it down his throat. (*pause*) I thought they'd just duff him up a bit. Honest.

59

CARTER: What did you do? Albert?
ALBERT: Nothing. What could I do?
CARTER: Did Eric know that Frank was my brother?
ALBERT: Yes. I told him.
CARTER: What did he say?
ALBERT: 'Good.'
Albert draws deeply on his cigarette.
They drove Frank away in a car.
CARTER: Is that all there is?
Albert nods.
Then that's it, Albert.
Carter takes something from his pocket. There's a loud click.
It's a knife.
ALBERT: Jack, for Christ's sake . . .
He falls to his knees.
CARTER: You knew what I'd do.
ALBERT: (*crying*) Yes, but listen. Christ, I didn't kill him.
Carter drives the knife into him with all his might.
CARTER: I know you didn't kill him. (*And again.*) I know you
didn't.
A ship's horn calls mournfully from the harbour. Albert leans
back. Blood seeps from his chest. He pitches forward,
twitches, and is dead.

INT. BETTING SHOP. DAY
Carter comes in from the back and walks calmly through to the
street. A blind man is at the counter placing a bet.

EXT. JETTY. TYNE FERRY. DAY
The Sunbeam waits in the car park. Eric, Con and Peter arrive in
the Land Rover and park behind it. They go down the gangplank
to the floating jetty. A ferry is chugging across the water.

INT. FERRY. DAY
Carter sits, watching the other passengers. A mother and two
young children take his attention. His look is tinted with regret
even remorse.

EXT. JETTY. DAY
As the ferry comes alongside, Eric, Con and Peter move up to the rail. The passengers disembark, leaving Carter standing alone. He's holding Con's handgun.
Eric, Con and Peter back slowly away to the steel shelters. Peter, impatient as ever, pulls a sawn-off automatic shooter from under his coat, cocks it and fires. Too late. Carter is already safely behind the ferry's superstructure. Eric shouts.
ERIC: No shooters. Cyril said no shooters, you stupid bastard.
PETER: Get stuffed.
He's reloading.
CON: Gerald wants to see him first.
PETER: Shut up.
Carter is listening to all this.
CARTER: (*shouting*) Are you coming in? Or do we piss about all day?
Eric laughs.
ERIC: You're finished, Jack. You know that, don't you? I've bloody finished you.
CARTER: Not till I'm dead, Eric.
Eric laughs.
ERIC: Oh, you've still got your sense of humour? Tell him how I've fixed him, Con.
CON: He's told Gerald about you and Anna.
ERIC: Didn't believe us at first, did he, Con? Then Peter talked to him.
PETER: Didn't even say goodbye. Just asked us to take you back – alive.
ERIC: He's probably talking to her right now. Are you still going to fancy her when Gerald's finished with her face?
Carter shows no emotion. Or are his eyes just that bit sadder? Peter lets rip again. Another window is shattered. Carter ducks back, allowing Peter time to board the ferry. Carter catches a glimpse of Peter as he climbs up the ferry's superstructure to the roof. By the time he heaves himself into position, Carter is waiting.
CARTER: Stay where you are, Peter.
Peter is helpless, clinging to the roof, unable to even raise his shooter.

PETER: (*screaming*) Don't.
> *There's a long pause while Carter looks at him, then he cold-bloodedly shoots. Peter is blown away. By the time he hits the deck, he's dead.*
> *Con and Eric panic. They run up the gangplank, safely out of range.*
ERIC: Carter, your car needs a wash.
> *Eric signals to the driver in the Land Rover to bump the Sunbeam into the water. Two hits and the task is done. Glenda's screams are lost as the river wraps itself around the sinking car.*
> *Carter watches impassively.*

EXT. BRUMBY'S RESTAURANT COMPLEX. DAY
Carter's hire car corners at speed into the high-rise car park.

INT. RESTAURANT. DAY
Brumby and two architects in a site meeting. Plans are laid out on a table.
BRUMBY: I don't want them cooking in here. You can put a hatch in that wall.
INTERIOR DECORATOR: Yes, it's all a question of . . .
> *The sound of a car screeching up the ramps interrupts him.*
BRUMBY: Who in Christ's name is that? It's a bloody madman.
> *He strides away to investigate.*

EXT. RESTAURANT. DAY
Brumby comes out to the top tier. On the floor below, Carter, unseen by Brumby, has parked and is now making for the concrete spiral staircase.

EXT. STAIRCASE. DAY
Brumby pounds down to the first level. Carter comes around the corner.
BRUMBY: Jack!
> *Carter slams his fist hard into his gut.*
CARTER: You shouldn't have shown the film to Frank.
BRUMBY: I had to. It was the only way I could get at them.

CARTER: You shouldn't have.

BRUMBY: Your brother was going to the police.

CARTER: You shit. You didn't have the guts to do it yourself, did you?

BRUMBY: They'd have killed me.

CARTER: They killed Frank instead.

BRUMBY: I didn't think they'd do it.

CARTER: How would you have liked it if it had been your daughter, eh? (*another punch*) Being poked in that film, eh? (*another punch*) What would you have done then? Slags like your Sandra can get away with it, can't they? The Doreens of this world can't, can they?

Carter sinks his fist into Brumby's face. Brumby is unconscious, slumped over the concrete side of the staircase, ten storeys up. Carter catches hold of his legs and tips him over.

EXT. BRUMBY'S RESTAURANT COMPLEX. DAY

Brumby's body spins down, out of sight. The sound of a crash on metal, followed by a persistent car horn.

EXT. STREET. DAY

Brumby's body has crushed the front of a family car. The driver's head has been jammed on to the horn. Bystanders rush to open the rear doors, lifting out the children.

EXT. ENTRANCE TO CAR PARK. DAY

Carter drives out. A moment later a police car, siren going, screeches around the corner into the building.

INT. RESTAURANT. DAY

The architects are waiting for Brumby to come back.

INTERIOR DECORATOR: It's very rude to disappear like that. (*pause*) Where can he possibly be?

The police car pulls up below them. They watch the officers pour out.

ARCHITECT: (*murmurs*) I have an awful feeling we're not going to get our fees on this job.

INT. BACK STREET POST OFFICE. EVENING.
It's a combined shop and post office. Carter is on the phone.
CARTER: The guy on the swing-bridge? (*pause*) OK.
Carter hangs up. He takes a can of film from his pocket and slips it into a large envelope.
At the counter two women are talking.
FIRST WOMAN: They don't know how it happened.
SECOND WOMAN: How far did he fall?
FIRST WOMAN: What did Betty say . . . Ninety floors, I think it was.
SECOND WOMAN: Really. Was he dead?
FIRST WOMAN: Oh, yes.
The envelope is passed across to the post office assistant. It is addressed to: Vice Squad, Scotland Yard, London SW1.
SECOND WOMAN: Better to go quick like that.

EXT. SWING-BRIDGE. EVENING.
The huge steel superstructure pivots on a large man-made island in the middle of the river.
On top is a structure not unlike a small lighthouse, from which a man operates the bridge. Carter climbs the outside ladder. A man waits for him at the top.
The man hands him a small cloth package. Carter opens it. Inside is heroin and a hypodermic. He wraps it up again and hands over an envelope. The man checks the money as Carter disappears down the outside ladder.

INT. BINGO HALL. NIGHT
The hall is crowded. The compere calls the numbers. The atmosphere is tense as the audience look at their cards. Someone calls, 'Bingo.' A buzz goes round the hall as everybody starts talking again.
Carter enters, surveying the audience. Eventually, his eyes alight on the person he's been looking for: Margaret. She's involved with a woman friend and doesn't see him.
The next game starts up.

EXT. BINGO HALL. NIGHT
*Crowds of people come pouring out. It's the end of the evening's
entertainment. Margaret walks out with her friend. Carter follows
them and turns up a side street.*

EXT. STEPS LEADING TO BACK STREET. NIGHT
*The place is deserted. Margaret and her friend descend the steps.
The clop of their high heels is the only sound. Carter follows
discreetly. At the bottom, Margaret and her friend chat for a
moment and part.*
Carter follows Margaret.

EXT. BACK ALLEY. NIGHT
*The clop of Margaret's shoes is heard in the distance. She appears.
Carter is following behind. He slips into another dark alley to
get ahead of her. As she reaches her home Carter's arm shoots
out from behind a pillar. It's holding Con's handgun.*
CARTER: I've come for you, Margaret.

INT. THE HEIGHTS. SITTING ROOM. NIGHT
*There's a big party going on. The music is loud. It's mainly rich-
looking middle-aged men and young dolly birds. Different things
are obviously going on in different rooms in the house. Dancing in
one room, blue movies in another, etc. Kinnear flits from one to
another. Eric Paice is on the phone. He puts the receiver down and
crosses to Kinnear.*
ERIC: Gerald Fletcher wants a word with you Cyril.
    Kinnear crosses to the telephone.
KINNEAR: Hello, Gerald.

EXT. VILLAGE TELEPHONE KIOSK. NIGHT
*Carter stands in the dimly lit kiosk with Margaret. The hire car is
parked alongside.*
CARTER: It's Carter. Listen carefully, you hairy-faced git. I've got
    the film and enough evidence to put you away for a long
    time. All it takes is one call to the police.

INT. THE HEIGHTS. SITTING ROOM. NIGHT
Kinnear listens.
KINNEAR: Really? *(pause)* So?

EXT. VILLAGE TELEPHONE KIOSK. NIGHT
Carter into phone.
CARTER: I'll do a simple deal with you. All I want is . . .

INT. THE HEIGHTS. SITTING ROOM. NIGHT
Kinnear is still listening to Carter. He looks over at Eric, who's fixing a drink.
KINNEAR: I see. I think that can be arranged.
    Kinnear continues listening.

INT. VILLAGE TELEPHONE KIOSK. NIGHT
Carter into phone.
CARTER: . . . but I don't want him there until six in the morning. OK? *(pause)* Right.
    Carter hangs up. He pushes Margaret towards the car.

INT. THE HEIGHTS. LIBRARY. NIGHT
The noise of the wild party is heard off. Eric comes into the room.
ERIC: You want something, Cyril?
KINNEAR: Yes, Eric. A word with you.

EXT. DESERTED WOOD. NIGHT
Headlights, through the thick trees, as Carter's car comes bouncing over rough ground.

INT. HIRE CAR. NIGHT
Carter stops in a clearing and leaves his headlights on. He turns to Margaret.
CARTER: Get out.
    Carter and Margaret get out. They appear in the beam of the headlights and move further into the wood.

EXT. WOOD. NIGHT
Carter and Margaret stop.
CARTER: Take your clothes off.
Margaret is confused.
Take your clothes off.
*Margaret does just that: coat, blouse, skirt. She goes to
remove her knickers.*
Keep your pants on. (*pause*) Lie down.
Again she obeys.
*He kneels on her, pinning her arms with his knees, then stuffs
a gag in her mouth.*
*He takes out the hypodermic, places it against her arm, and
injects the heroin into her. She struggles, her eyes moving
frantically about. She screams, but its muffled by the gag.
Carter holds her down and she quickly goes under.*
*Carter removes the gag. He stands, picks her up and walks
into the darkness with Margaret in his arms.*

INT. THE HEIGHTS. LIBRARY. NIGHT
*Kinnear is alone, speaking on the telephone quietly. The party is
still going on.*
KINNEAR: I want you to listen very carefully. Jack Carter. (*pause*)
You know what he looks like?

INT. HOTEL BEDROOM. NIGHT
A bedside light is on. A man in bed is listening on the phone.
MAN: Yes.
*He taps his cigarette against the ashtray. On his middle finger
is a large ring with the initial 'J' on it. He listens until the line
goes dead.*
*The woman beside him stirs. He stubs out the cigarette and
switches off the light. Darkness.*

EXT. THE HEIGHTS. DAWN
*Eric comes out of the front door. Inside the party is still in
progress. He gets into a Cadillac and drives off.*

EXT. COUNTRY ROAD. DAWN
Carter is parked where he can see the drive up to Kinnear's house.
The Cadillac appears and swings on to the road.
There's the sound of a phone being dialled.
CARTER: (*voice-over*) Police.

EXT. THE HEIGHTS. DAWN
A long line of police cars move slowly up the drive, followed by a
police bus. They park by the front door and around fifty
policemen pour out. They move silently around the building. A
chief constable opens the front door and walks in.

INT. THE HEIGHTS. DAWN
The police move through the house and grounds. In the bedrooms
they find groups of people in bed together. The men in particular
protest and are obviously concerned about being identified. The
police find evidence of drugs, pornography and so on.
Outside, police are combing the grounds. In the long grass leading
down to the lake they find women's clothes. They follow the trail
until they discover a woman floating naked, face downwards, in
the lake. A policeman with waders goes in and pulls her to the
side. As others heave her out, we see that it's Margaret.

EXT. THE HEIGHTS. DAWN
The house is surrounded by police measuring and photographing,
and outside the house are police cars and ambulances.
The lawn is crowded with the party crowd. In the early-morning
light, they look like dolls.
Kinnear comes out of the front door with two plain-clothes officers
and gets in a police car. Sirens going, it comes down the short drive
to the gate.

INT. HIRE CAR. DAWN
Carter is driving along a coast road. The sea and a wide beach lie
on his right. Long rows of houses are to his left.
The sun is still low. It's very quiet. He arrives at a harbour and
drives on until he reaches the end of a vast wooden jetty running
out into the estuary. It's a coal loader for tankers.

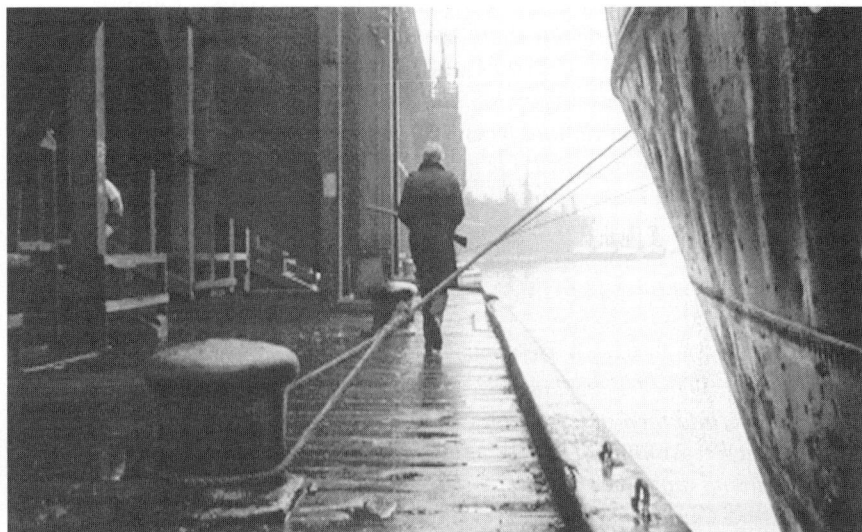

This jetty is very high, a complex of wooden staves and pillars, interwoven with steps and gangways. On its top tier is a complex of railway lines, signals and black coal chutes.

EXT. COAL JETTY. DAWN
Carter parks his car and picks up the shotgun and a bottle of Scotch off the back seat. He get out and walks over to the jetty and along a lower gangway. At the far end, a man is standing. It's Eric Paice. Eric turns around abruptly. He sees Carter and disappears up the nearest stairway. Carter follows.
At the top he stops to listen, but can see and hear only the harbour waters lapping below.
Carter looks back to the coal jetty, just in time to see Eric scamper down to the level below. Eric sprints for the roadway. Carter waits and then starts running directly above him.
Eric keeps running. Carter stays always overhead. He's playing cat and mouse with Eric.
CARTER: (*calling out*) You couldn't win an egg and spoon race, Eric.
ERIC: (*wheezing*) Sod off.
   Paice darts down another staircase to ground level and makes for the roadway. Carter stops above the roadway. Below, Paice makes for the parked car. Carter holds the gun up. Eric stops and looks up.
CARTER: Stay away from the car or I'll blow you apart.
   Eric darts under the jetty. Carter runs on down the steps. He can see Eric scampering along the row of cottages towards the beach. Carter starts after him.

EXT. BEACH. EARLY DAY
Eric runs out on to the beach. The only sounds are his feet pounding the pebbles and his hurtful panting.
In the distance, factory chimneys belch out smoke.
Carter appears. For a moment he watches Eric stumbling along at the far end of the beach. He climbs down to the beach and starts running.

EXT. BEACH. EARLY DAY
Carter is gaining on Eric rapidly. Eric looks round and panics. He stumbles and falls over.
He gets to his feet quickly and disappears round the headland. Carter follows.

EXT. BEACH. EARLY DAY
On the other side of the headland, the scene is extraordinary. The deserted beach is like the edge of the world. The sand is black as far as the eye can see. It's littered with rubbish. Several old lorries are sunk deep in the sand. High, grass-covered cliffs flank it on the left. It's deserted.
In the distance, a continuous line of giant black buckets move, like cable-cars, out to sea, before they deposit their load of coal slag and move inland again. The coal mine itself is inland, hidden away behind the cliffs. The sea, like the sand, is black as it crashes on to the shore.
Eric is half-way along the beach, struggling in the mud. Carter closes on him.

EXT. BEACH. EARLY DAY
Eric nears the line of buckets and cuts inland towards the mine. Carter has nearly caught up. The buckets grind and crash as they move along the cable.
Eric scrambles up the narrow valley down which the coal slag travels. He is panting horribly. Carter is close on his heels.
Near the top, where the buckets are practically at ground level, Eric stumbles and falls. He is too exhausted to get up.
Carter stands over him.
CARTER: (*panting slightly*) Stand up, Eric. Stand up.
    Eric just manages it. Carter pulls the bottle of Scotch out of his pocket.
    I bet you could use a drink, could you, Eric?
    He throws the bottle to Eric.
    Eh? Have a drink.
ERIC: Still got your sense of humour.
    Eric takes the cap off and looks at Carter. He's in a terrible state.

76

CARTER: Drink up, Eric. Drink up. I want you to drink all of that. Do you understand? Drink up. Just like it was with my brother, Frank. Go on, son. Drink up.
Eric pours the whisky into his mouth. It spills over and runs down his face.
Drink up, Eric.
Eric begins to stagger about.
It was you who poured it down him. Eh, Eric?
Eric takes a breather and looks pathetically at Carter. No mercy there.
Did you all have a good laugh, eh? Did you have a good laugh when he was spewing it up?
The whisky is pouring all over Eric's face and suit. It's disgusting to watch. Suddenly, he retches, but nothing comes up.
Drink it! Drink it! Did you all pass the bottle round after the car went over the top?
Eric is choking.
Don't stop, Eric.
Carter leans forward and with his free hand lifts the bottle up to Eric's mouth again. In the other, he holds the shotgun.
Eric chokes and retches. Carter has seen enough.
Goodbye, Eric.
Carter raises the butt of the gun and brings it down on Eric's head.

EXT. BEACH. EARLY DAY
Eric's body, loaded on to a a coal bucket, moves off on it's final journey. Carter, laughing, walks beside it, gun riding on his shoulder. The bucket shudders and grinds as it moves along the cable. Eric's body moves of on its final journey. It reaches the end of the line, where an automatic catch tilts it. Eric's body drops into the sea. The coal slag follows in a cloud of black dust. The waves pass over and everything is gone.
Carter stands for a moment, turns and walks back along the beach. He stops, looks at the shotgun, and decides to get rid of it.

EXT. CLIFF TOP. EARLY MORNING

Below, Carter moves slowly by the edge of the sea. He raises the shotgun to throw it away. High on the clifftop a rifle and telescopic lens line up on Carter. A finger curls around the trigger. On the middle finger of the same hand is a large gold ring with the letter 'J' engraved upon it. It is the man Kinnear contacted after sending Eric to his death.

The finger tightens on the trigger and pulls it. There's a quiet, whooshing sound. Carter drops to the ground.

EXT. BEACH. EARLY MORNING

Carter lies on the beach. The waves lap around his head. A small trickle of blood pours out of a hole in his temple. He's dead.

EXT. CLIFF TOP. EARLY MORNING

Kinnear's hit man coolly dismantles his rifle.

He carefully wraps it in a cloth fishing-rod carrier. He walks off and is soon lost as he drops out of sight.

Brute Force

Get Carter is the apex of post-sixties British crime films, the
gleaming pinnacle of a slag heap. Written and directed by Mike
Hodges, who had a sleeper hit this past summer with *Croupier*
but whose career has otherwise proved erratic, the 1971 gangland
classic is an icon of male fantasy-fulfilment. Never mind Michael
Caine's Oscars, it was surely *Get Carter* that Tony Blair was
watching at 10 Downing Street when he decided to knight the
erstwhile Smithfield porter, a perfect emblem, if ever there were
one, of working-class advancement. And yet Hodges's film, more
a penetrating character study of a sensitive, delusional psychopath
than a celebration of underworld chic, has been largely
misinterpreted. It's time for a reappraisal.

In 1996, *Loaded* magazine, the flagship of the British 'new lad'
culture, serialized a comic-strip version of *Get Carter*. It was a
different type of consecration for a British crime film that had
been regularly spoken of as 'seminal' because of the presumed
influence of its unflinching violence on John MacKenzie's *The
Long Good Friday* and Neil Jordan's *Mona Lisa*. *Get Carter* was
subsequently rereleased in Britain last June (a week before
Croupier, Hodges's latest), and its screenplay was published for
the first time and packaged with an issue of the British Film
Institute monthly *Sight and Sound*. The shotgun brandished by
Michael Caine's Jack Carter rematerialized in the brace of antique
rifles that serve as *Lock, Stock and Two Smoking Barrels'*
MacGuffin, while *The Limey*, for all its liberal quoting of *Poor
Cow*, clearly took its revenge motif and its melancholy from *Get
Carter*.

Expressly English in its vernacular, *Get Carter* has never meant
much over here [in the USA], though it'll hopefully get some play
this fall when the long-gestating – and potentially redundant –
Sylvester Stallone remake arrives. Even in Britain, *Get Carter*
languished for two decades, but it's easy to see why the cult
around the film blossomed in the mid-nineties. It was a period of

cultural realignment – a post-feminist swinging back of the pendulum – that redefined the right of the young British male to be laddish but not boorish, sexist but not misogynistic. Symbols included the rock band Oasis and (until he beat up his wife) the boozing soccer star Paul Gascoigne.

There was, however, no contemporary British movie star with whom the boys could identify, and so the mantle fell on Caine – not the affable 60-year-old international movie star, but the Caine of *Get Carter*, who announces his cool by snapping his fingers at a barman and demanding his pint 'in a thin glass,' has phone sex with Britt Ekland's gangster's girlfriend (clad for the occasion in black silk lingerie – a *Loaded* spread come to life), and actual sex with his randy landlady and a moll who doubled as a porn actress. Characterized by film critics as 'amoral' in his disposal of Newcastle upon Tyne's gangland scum, Carter was a hybrid of Clint Eastwood's Man With No Name at his most ruthless and Alfie, Caine's troubled Cockney casanova in the 1966 film of that name.

The notion that *Get Carter*'s appeal is to unreconstructed male fantasies of sexual irresponsibility, avenging-angel brutality, and the fastidiousness of the practiced beer drinker is limiting, however. It is genuinely sexy for a British film of the period (for a British film of any period), but it's as doomy as Dickens' *Dombey and Son*. It's also a thriller altogether lacking in tension. Resembling British TV cop dramas like *The Sweeney*, it's more televisual than cinematic. Carter's quips – 'You're a big man, but you're in bad shape. With me, it's a full-time job' – are eminently quotable, but calculated. And the acting is nonchalant, though Caine's is deceptively so. Nobody works up much of a sweat in the film, beyond the reliable Glynn Edwards as the unlikely porn actor Carter knifes in a bookie's backyard. Once seen, though, *Get Carter* burns inextinguishably in your memory – and you rather wish it would go out.

Adapted from Ted Lewis's terse (and, at the time, unpublished) novel *Jack's Return Home*, *Get Carter* was relocated by first-time writer-director Hodges from Lewis's anonymous steel-town setting, where all but the opening scene takes place, to Newcastle in England's north-east. This enabled Hodges to inscribe in the film Newcastle's so-called Fruit Machine Murder of 1968. One Angus Sibbet had been shot for creaming the profits off a rigged one-arm bandit business; Michael Luvaglio and Dennis Stafford were tried for Sibbet's murder and convicted. Their boss, Vincent Landa, Luvaglio's brother, subsequently bolted to Majorca. In the film, Brian Mosley, formerly a regular on the classic prime-time soap *Coronation Street*, was cast against type as Brumby, a small-time fruit machine supplier being squeezed by the gangster and pornographer Kinnear, who has had Carter's brother Frank rubbed out. Kinnear, effete and reptilian, was played by the playwright John Osborne; Kinnear's palatial country residence was the actual house that Landa abandoned when he fled. You can feel the vibes.

Frank was murdered because, having seen his teenage daughter Doreen raped in one of Kinnear's films, he had threatened to blow the whistle. Brumby is implicated in both Frank's murder and the porn racket and so Carter tosses him off the roof of a building he is redeveloping. Alerted by the police sirens, one of the two (indubitably bent) architects working for Brumby says to the other, 'I have an awful feeling we're not going to get our fees on this job.' It's not a throwaway line. Hodges, who had worked on ITV's investigative documentary series *World in Action*, sensed during location scouting that crime in Newcastle extended way beyond the syndicates. He could not have known that, by the late seventies, the local council would be enmeshed in a vast civic redevelopment scandal, although in *Get Carter* the aura of small crimes that are harbingers of general corruption is palpable, like a drop of pus suddenly noticed on a shirt cuff. It's the same mood that Robert Towne captured in *Chinatown*.

The documentarist in Hodges didn't want to gussy up this milieu: rain and neon could have drained it of malignancy and sentimentalized the sadness that engulfs Carter – sick to start with, judging by his compulsivity and pill-popping – as he goes about his business. So Hodges brought a flat, emotionless *mise-en-scène* to Newcastle's seedy pubs and clubs, its back-to-back terraced housing, its waterfront, and the polluted beach where Carter chases Paice (Ian Hendry), Kinnear's pimp, to a final reckoning. The result was a film devoid of visual poetry, as drab and prosaic as other Newcastle-based films, including Mike Figgis's *Stormy Monday* and Paul Anderson's *Shopping*, are garishly stylized. And, of course, that absence of style comprises a style – monotonous dankness – that's in keeping with the film's dystopic vision.

Structurally, if not stylistically, *Get Carter* is a quintessential noir. The film begins with a scene in which a London hoodlum, his wife Anna (Ekland), his brother, and Carter watch a pornographic slideshow in a penthouse suite. But the actual opening shot shows Carter, bored by the smut, standing gloomily by the window – a shot that presages Robert Mitchum's Philip Marlowe at the beginning of *Farewell, My Lovely*. And it's the Raymond Chandler novel that that neglected Dick Richards's film was based on that Carter reads on the train going north in the following scene. Sitting across from him in the compartment is his eventual assassin.

In classic noir fashion, as Carter thrusts himself into Newcastle's labyrinthine underworld – with Circes and Beatrices laying in wait – his physical journey mirrors that which he takes into his own, private underworld. The film's action constantly suggests that Carter has constructed his own psychosexual reality: there's a repertory theater in his mind showing two kinds of films, softcore and hardcore. The phone sex, for example, is depicted as a softcore masturbation fantasy. Ekland's Anna is more of a phantom than a flesh-and-blood woman in love with Carter; his belief that they are going to run off to South America together is a pipe dream. Similarly, when the gangland floozy, Glenda (Geraldine Moffat), rescues Carter from Kinnear's heavies, she presents herself as 'a fairy godmother, all of your own'; their subsequent fuck is preceded by more jokey softcore foreplay, in which she fondles her sports car's gearstick. The implication is that all this is in Carter's head. Even the sex he has with his landlady has a schoolboy fantasy element, charged as it is with Oedipal meaning (landlady = mother).

If Carter's womanizing isn't as overtly neurotic as Alfie's, the madonnas and whores he encounters symbolize the return of the repressed that 'Jack's return home' has set in motion. Carter is guilt-ridden. When we learn he slept with Frank's wife and is probably Doreen's real father, we realize why he left 'this craphole' in the first place and why, like *The Searchers'* Ethan Edwards and *Taxi Driver'*s Travis Bickle, he is fixated on purging. The only woman he doesn't have some sort of sex with is the strictly taboo Margaret, Frank's ex-girlfriend and the surrogate mother who procured Doreen for the porno film. So Carter cold-bloodedly executes her, injecting her with heroin before dumping her in the stream near Kinnear's estate. Is that amoral or acceptable, given Margaret's corrupting influence? It certainly indicates that Carter is mad.

Reading this, you may think it's time to get Carter off the couch and return him to the world of casual slaughter and easy sex that his public want him to occupy. But then Carter has become aware of his psychopathy during the film and, like Ethan, has nowhere to go, which is why Hodges kills him off without compunction. Concealing Carter's anguish and his fatalism under a veneer of jocularity – the film's tagline, as spoken by Paice, is both question and statement: 'Still got your sense of humour [?]' – Caine gave the subtlest performance of his career. The film's psychological and mythic resonances urge us to think about it as a great British film – which is something more than just the greatest British crime film. Given the recent spate of *Lock, Stock* knockoffs in Britain, it is proof that, as the northern English saying goes, 'Where there's muck, there's occasional diamonds.'

Graham Fuller
Film Comment,
2000

Review of *Get Carter*

An underrated, seldom-mentioned noir masterpiece, Mike Hodges's *Get Carter* is the shiny suit of British cinema. Carter (Caine) is a London gangster who finds out his brother has been offed back home in Newcastle. We get a brief glimpse of Carter's chums and digs in London before he hies himself off to the North; we know he's screwing Ekland, who's mistress of the local boss, and that he's a well-respected tough nut. The color's dark, murky in London, and in Newcastle it gets watery, runny, and bland. England looks bleak here, and its inhabitants, exemplified by Carter and company, seedy and nasty. It's the lower depths striving to look respectable and it doesn't work.

They know it, too. The moment Carter sets foot in town the Newcastle hoods are on his case. He rents a room from a whorish landlady, whom he taunts and excites by making a phone call to Ekland in her presence, instructing Ekland to masturbate while he coos into the phone. This disconcerts not only the landlady – who, of course, Carter soon beds – but Ekland's boyfriend, who catches her at it. The movie is full of this kinky stuff. When the Newcastle mob boys roust Carter as he's having it off with the landlady, he grabs a double-barreled shotgun from under the bed and marches the thugs out into the street in front of the house without bothering to put on his clothes. A parade is going by at the time and the old woman on her porch next door keels over at the sight. Carter doesn't flinch, just makes certain the baddies exit. There's also an aborted sex scene with Carter and the old lady of the local crime boss – seedily portrayed by British playwright John Osborne – whereat Carter discovers his niece, who may in reality be his daughter, in a porno film produced by the mob.

Carter's brother's been whacked by Osborne's guys, obviously, because he knew too much, even though he was a small-time bloke. Carter figures it out right away but has to go through a series of evening-up exercises like locking Osborne's mistress in the trunk of her own car just before the brutes unwittingly dump it in the river. She's no bloody good, Carter's expression says, let her go. It's a cold-shot movie, with Caine cruel, clever, and deliberate. *Get Carter* is the movie Peckinpah's version of Jim Thompson's *The Getaway* should have been. McQueen wasn't the actor Caine is, though; he was less subtle and gave everything away with that hang-dog look. Caine has more than two expressions, that's the real difference.

Hodges has the action raw and quick: Carter's either fucking, shooting, throwing somebody off a roof, or observing. You can see his brain registering and computing and plotting. After he's gone too far, gotten too close, Osborne finds a way to have Carter killed, but by the time it happens, on a lonely beach – Carter having accomplished what he came for really – it's already over. We don't *like* Carter – he's a sociopathic, perverse murderer – but we respect his lack of pretense. He may not like himself, either, but he's got his self-respect. Life is for shit, he seems to be thinking, but there's a certain fascination in watching people try to wipe it off.

Barry Gifford
from *The Devil Thumbs a Ride*
and *Other Unforgettable Films,*
1988

Review of *Pulp* and *Get Carter*

Outside of Peckinpah's films, in which, at least before *The Getaway*, the violence has always been used with a serious intention to disturb, the movie which seemed to me the most disturbingly violent of those of the past few years was an icily skillful British film, *Get Carter*. A gangster film, with Michael Caine as a vicious thug avenging the death of his brother by a series of murders as he works his way toward the man he's after, what made it so disturbing was not the violence itself, ugly as that was, but the utter affectlessness with which it was presented; it was perhaps the most affectlessly violent film since *Kiss Me Deadly*, but without an equivalent of the allegorical framework by which the violence in *Kiss Me Deadly* is given meaning. No sympathy is asked for the avenger or his victims, nor are we allowed to take any vicarious pleasure in his successful completion of his task; minutes after he completes it, he, too, is killed, by a disinterested hireling. Nor is there even a suggestion that this final twist is intended as a slap in the audience's face, in the way that such thwarting of an audience's expectations in Hitchcock's films is, as a deliberate assault on the spectators' sensibilities, at least an acknowledgment of them.

The writer and director of *Get Carter*, Mike Hodges, has now made another film with Michael Caine, and, if, short of the work of the best directors, there has been a more impressively versatile one-two punch in films, I can't recall it. *Pulp*, too, is a thriller, but a thriller in a very special vein: something like *Beat the Devil*, if not as good, and something like *Gumshoe*, but better. (Indeed, unless I'm mistaken, it even features in a small role, the only other in which I've seen him, the actor who played the Arab chieftan in *Beat the Devil*, who when told that Humphrey Bogart, Robert Morley, and company have landed clandestinely on his country's shores to sell vacuum cleaners, utters the memorable line, 'Ah, hut to hut, I suppose.' In *Pulp*, as the head of a typing pool who has been stimulated by a pornographic novel his staff is preparing, he speaks, to the book's author, a few other memorable lines: 'You have my card. Don't hesitate to touch me.')

Mickey King, the film's narrator-protagonist, played by a poker-faced Michael Caine in a performance scarcely less good than that of Albert Finney in *Gumshoe*, is the author of that novel, a successful writer of pulp fiction (*The Organ Grinder, My Gun Is Long*, etc.) under such pseudonyms as Guy Strange, Les Behan, Paul R. Cumming, and as the promising new literary discoveries from Egypt and Algeria, O. R. Gann and S. Odomy. Summoned to ghost-write the memoirs of an ex-star of Hollywood gangster movies now living in retirement in the same Mediterranean country as the writer, he suddenly finds his employer assassinated, and himself the target of assassins' bullets as the presumed recipient of the star's secrets of a covered-up scandal. Though in fact the deceased star hadn't confided in his biographer, the latter now launches an investigation into the matter on his own to discover the identity of his intended killer before it's too late; but he uncovers the facts of the case only to find himself at the end, immobilized by a leg wound, the unwilling house guest, presumably for his lifetime, of the guilty party, the country's 'New Front' political leader, at whose estate the writer spends his days composing and reciting a pulp fantasy of revenge on his 'host' to which nobody listens.

All this is recounted in a style half pulp itself, and half witty parody of it. 'The old man's headed for the big sleep,' the movie star's bodyguard tells the ghost writer, as though the former had read too many detective novels; 'then I knew he'd get his pictures in the paper,' the writer remarks of a character he has just found murdered, and later he describes the series of events in which he finds himself embroiled as being 'like a pornographic photograph: difficult to figure out who was doing what, and to whom.' At the movie star's Art Deco villa, a wizened old woman in black dress and shawl sits and stares into the swimming pool ('Has mama eaten this week?' her son inquires); and when the star is killed (by a man disguised as a priest, which occasions a police line-up of priests), and his sculpted sarcophagus installed in a mausoleum with stained-glass windows depicting him in his most famous film roles, there is a juke box featuring excerpts from his films' soundtracks outside, and the mother is forever provided with coins with which to play it. A clue from a clairvoyant ('He was wearing a dirty mackintosh. Clairvoyants usually do.') leads to an Antonioniesque ghost town of the old and maimed, and eventually to a second narrow escape from assassination ('Remember that thou art pulp, and unto pulp thou shalt return,' the writer eulogizes over the mangled corpse of his hired would-be killer). But his escape from being silenced is short-lived. As we last see him, his leg in a cast, reading aloud while his captor shoots boar in a pit ('Where *do* you get your ideas from, Mickey?' his one remaining listener asks as she leaves him), he is wistfully exclaiming, 'I'll get the bastards yet!' and then, with more conviction, 'Ooh, I wish my leg didn't itch.'

This column hasn't gone in much for consumer guidance; here is some: see *Pulp*. You may have a hard time doing this, since the film, after opening in San Francisco, unreviewed, on the bottom half of a double bill with a Charles Bronson movie (this despite a cast including, along with Caine, Lizabeth Scott, Lionel Stander, and Mickey Rooney, in a flamboyantly amusing performance) is thus far having its only New York performance as part of a limited engagement of a series of movies (works by Arrabal, etc.) reputed to be without commercial possibilities. That the, I think, very real commercial possibilities of *Pulp* can't be seen constitutes probably the biggest gaffe in film distribution since the mishandling of the Marlon Brando-Gillo Pontecorvo film, *Burn!*; the idea that film distributors have a grasp of at least the commercial side of movies is one of the great undying myths, like that of *Time* magazine's at least getting its facts straight. But then, when you withhold a 'risky' movie from distribution, or simply dump it unadvertised into release, you are, of course, always right, since you're dealing in self-fulfilling prophecy.

Try to see *Pulp* without my having to tell you that it's great or a masterpiece when it isn't, or even that it's unfailingly good. (Most of the less good jokes are clustered near the beginning.) But though it would be well worth seeing merely because of its being a hugely funny entertainment, it isn't simply that either. I don't know anything about Mike Hodges, its writer-director; to judge from the hard clarity of his style, my guess is that he's had considerable experience in film-making before, perhaps for television, although *Get Carter* is his first credited feature. Impressive, however, as is the diversity between that film and this, no less impressive is how much similarity that diversity masks. In a curious way, though I probably wouldn't have said this about either without having seen both, the two films now strike me as peculiarly if unspecifically political in character, involving, as they do, corruption in high places, and the sexual exploitation, in both, of a lower-class girl by those in power. And both films portray the insurmountable frustration of trying to call the powerful to account. Don't get me wrong; *Get Carter* resolutely eschews 'significance,' and, like the rest of the film, the ending of *Pulp* is lightly done and very funny. And yet somehow the two films, taken together, seem to me to take on an added resonance, and finally to issue in a single, distinctive cry of impotent rage.

William Pechter
'Remember Thou Art Pulp', *Commentary*,
1972

Biography

Born in Bristol, Avon, on 29 July 1932, Hodges qualified as an accountant, but worked as a postman, farm labourer and bed salesman before completing two years of National Service in the Royal Navy. In 1957, he went to work for the American company Teleprompter and this introduction to the world of television tempted him to try his luck at freelance writing. One of his successful scripts, *Some Will Cry Murder*, enabled him to take up writing full-time.

During 1962–3 he was editor of the religious series *The Sunday Break*. He then became a producer/director for Granada's *World in Action* in 1963–4. Among the numerous programmes he compiled for this groundbreaking current affairs series was a profile on presidential candidate Barry Goldwater and one of the first reports on Vietnam.

From 1965 to 1966, Hodges became producer of the arts series *Tempo* originated by Kenneth Tynan, and he was responsible for profiles on such respected artists as Jacques Tati, Jean-Luc Godard and Orson Welles. He followed this by writing, directing and producing two Thames Television thrillers, *Suspect* and *Rumour*.

Get Carter was Hodges's directorial movie debut and he also scripted the film. Starring Michael Caine, the 1971 gangster thriller had a toughness unusual in British films of the time and was both a critical and a box-office success. Caine starred again for him in *Pulp*, the 1972 offbeat black comedy also written by Hodges. He then made his Hollywood directing debut in 1974 with *The Terminal Man*, based on Michael Crichton's best-selling science-fiction novel. In 1978, Hodges co-wrote the horror-film *Damien: Omen II* and in 1980 directed the comic-strip spoof *Flash Gordon*.

After the 1983 television movie *Missing Pieces*, Hodges's next project was *Squaring the Circle*, playwright Tom Stoppard's searing television drama about the Solidarity Movement in Poland. The 1984 film won many awards, including the New

York Critics' Prize and the New York Television Festival's Gold Award, and it marked the first time Hodges teamed up with Voytek Roman, his future production designer, in *Black Rainbow*. The next year saw the release of the science-fiction comedy *Morons from Outer Space*, starring the popular British funnymen Griff Rhys Jones and Mel Smith. The same year Hodges directed the television movie *Florida Straits*. Filmed on location in North Carolina, it was this project which laid the creative seeds for *Black Rainbow*.

In 1987, Hodges directed the controversial Jack Higgins IRA thriller *A Prayer for the Dying*, starring Mickey Rourke, Bob Hoskins and Alan Bates. He won the Best Screenplay Award for *Black Rainbow* at the 22nd Sitges Fantasy Film Festival in October 1989.

From 1993 to 1995, Mike Hodges directed two two-part serials, *Dandelion Dead*, which was transmitted on LWT, starring Michael Kitchen and Sarah Miles, and *The Healer*, scripted by G. F. Newman, shown on the BBC.

In 1998 he teamed up with an old friend, Paul Mayersberg (*A Man Who Fell to Earth, Merry Christmas Mr Lawrence, Eureka*) and directed *Croupier*, starring Clive Owen.

He has also written two plays *Soft Shoe Shuffle* (1985 Lyric, Hammersmith) and *Shooting Stars* and *Other Heavenly Pursuits* (2001 Old Red Lion, Islington).

Filmography

1958   **Once upon a Time** (children's TV series) writer
1962   **The Sunday Break**
        (TV series on religious topics) editor
1963 **Rave!** (TV series, tx 29.6.63–27.7.63) script
1963–5 **World in Action**
        (TV doc) producer/director; including:
            Goldwater (tx 30.6.1964)
            The Flip Side (tx 22.9.1964)
            US Elections (tx 29.9.1964
            Canada (tx 6.10.1964) collaboration with
            Douglas Keay
            Vietnam (tx 3.11.1964)
            State of the Unions (tx 1.12.1964)
1965–6 **Tempo** (TV arts magazine)
        producer/director, including profiles of
            Harold Pinter (tx 3.10.1965)
            Jean-Luc Godard (tx 10.10.1965)
            Michael Tippett (tx 17.10.1965)
            Alain Robbe-Grillet (tx 24.10.1965)
            Orson Welles (tx 31.10.1965)
            Andre Courreger tx 7.10.1965)
        Tempo series on 'Entertainers':
            A Guided Tour of Zero Mostel
            (tx 23.1.1966)
            Never Whistle in a Dressing Room
            (tx 30.1.1966)
            A Tale of Two Talents (tx 6.2.1966)
            You've Got a Nerve (tx 13.2.1966)
            Stop It, You're Killing Me (tx 20.2.1966)
            Don't Let the Wig Fool You, Mate
            (tx 27.2.1966)
            Meet the Duke (tx 6.3.1966)
        'Tempo International':
            In Cold Blood (tx 1.5.1966)
            Tativille (tx 8.5.1966)
            Girodias Rides Again (tx 15.5.1966)

Blood, Sweat and Champagne
(tx 22.5.1966)
Jazz in Wonderland (tx 29.5.1966)
The Offenders (tx 5.6.1966)
It Happened in Paris (tx 12.6.1966)
The Image-Wizards (tx 19.6.1966)
David, Moffett and Ornette (tx 26.6.1966)
When the War Was Over (tx 3.7.1966)
The Pursuit of Nancy Mitford (tx 10.7.1966)

1967   **New Tempo**
(TV arts magazine) executive producer/director:
The Information Explosion (tx 1.1.1967)
Nostalgia (tx 8.1.1967)
Noise (tx 15.1.1967)
Violence (tx 22.1.1967)
Heroes (tx 29.1.1967)
Expendability (a.k.a. **Disposability**, tx
5.2.1967)
Stimulants (tx 12.2.1967)
Leisure (tx 19.2.1967)

1968   **The Tyrant King** (children's TV serial, tx
3.10.1968–7.11.1968
director/producer

1969   **Playhouse: Suspect** (TV, tx 17.11.1969)
director/producer/screenplay

1970   **Playhouse: Rumour** (TV, tx 2.3.70)
director/producer/screenplay

1971   **Get Carter** director/screenplay

1972   **Pulp** director/screenplay/production
company, Klinger-Caine-Hodges
The Frighteners: The Manipulators
(TV, tx 28.7.1972) director/screenplay

1974   **The Terminal Man**
director/producer/screenplay

1978   **Damien: Omen II**
co-screenplay: also uncredited original
director, replaced by Don Taylor

1980   **Flash Gordon** director

1983   **And the Ship Sails On/E la nava va**
(director Federico Fellini)
Dubbing director of English version
Missing Pieces

(TV movie, tx 14.5.1983) director
The Hitchhiker: WGOD
(episode of TV series, tx 26.11.75) director

1984   **Squaring the Circle** (TV, tx 31.5.1984) director

1985   **Morons from Outer Space** director

1986   **Florida Straits** (TV movie, tx 26.10.1986)
director

1987   **A Prayer for the Dying** director

1989   **Black Rainbow** director/screenplay

1990   **Film Club** (TV, tx date unknown) discussing
Paolo and Vittorio Taviani's film *Kaos* (1984)

1994   **Dandelion Dead** (TV, tx 6+20.9.1994) director
The Lifeforce Experiment/The Breakthrough
(TV, tx 16.4.94, director Piers Haggard)
screenplay (written 1992)
Close Up (TV, ep 4.10.1995)
talking about Satyajit Ray's *Pather Panchali*

1998   **Croupier** director

screenplays (unrealized)

1975   **Mid-Atlantic**

1976   **The Chilean Club**

1977   **Spare Parts**

1978   **Blood and Thunder**
Say Goodnight, Lilian – Goodnight

1983   **Buried Alive**

1986   **A Cuckoo's Child**

1988   **Midnight Shakes the Memory**
(based on Marc Blitzstein's opera 'The Cradle
Will Rock', finally separately adapted/
directed by Tim Robbins 1999)

1991   **Tiger Rag**
Maiden

1996   **Acid Casuals**
(based on the novel by Nicholas Blincoe)

1999   **Grist**

A CLOCKWORK ORANGE
Stanley Kubrick

This unique illustrated screenplay contains over 800 still images from the film selected by Stanley Kubrick when the film was first released in 1972.

As Kubrick comments in his introduction, 'I have always wondered if there might be a more meaningful way to present a book about a film. To make, as it were, a complete, graphic representation of the film, cut by cut, with the dialogue printed in the proper place in relation to the cuts, so that within the limits of still-photographs and words, an accurate (and I hope interesting) record of a film might be available to anyone who had a bit more curiosity than just knowing what happened in the last reel. This book represents that attempt.'

Paperback – 208mm x 136mm   192pp 1 901680 47 9   **£14.99**

October 2001

THE ITALIAN JOB
Troy Kennedy Martin

'You're only supposed to blow the bloody doors off'

The immortal lines of Charlie Croker as he prepares for an audacious bullion robbery in Turin during the late sixties. This highly quotable screenplay has never before been available in print yet it holds a special place in the history of classic British cinema. Written by the originator of *Z Cars* and subsequent writer the BBC's *The Edge of Darkness*, it remains a classic caper.

Paperback – 216mm x 135mm   164pp 1 901680 33 9   **£7.99**

Order online at www.screenpress.co.uk